Workbook for Wheelock's Latin Grammar

HARPERCOLLINS COLLEGE OUTLINE

Workbook for Wheelock's Latin Grammar

2nd Edition

Paul D. Comeau
New Mexico State University

HarperPerennial
A Division of HarperCollinsPublishers

An American BookWorks Corporation Production

Project Manager: William Hamill

ISBN: 0-06-467171-2

92 93 94 95 96 ABW/RRD 10 9 8 7 6 5 4 3

Contents

Preface

This workbook, ancillary to Wheelock's Latin Grammar, *has been developed especially for high-school and college students and any private-study individuals who, as a result of a somewhat limited linguistic experience, may desire the extra auxiliary guidance and discipline provided by the written exercises of this book. The student should begin by studying the material in a given chapter of Wheelock's* Latin Grammar *and should then review and strengthen such study by writing out the fill-in exercises on that lesson. Having mastered the text of each chapter, the student will then be well prepared to read with pleasure the* Sententiae Antiquae, *which are the most important and rewarding part of each chapter.*

Each chapter is organized under the following headings.

OBJECTIVES

This section sets forth what the students are expected to accomplish in the study of each chapter.

GRAMMAR

Forms and their meanings; usages. Note the admonition in each chapter to *Memorize Paradigms (Models) and Vocabularies by Repeating Them Aloud.* This method, though admittedly somewhat tedious, is crucial for the successful study of Latin since one can thus learn through the *two* senses of *sight* and *hearing*.

DRILL

This provides written practice with individual words, groups of words, and short sentences in order to use the rules and the vocabulary of the chapter and thus to form a sort of transition between the *Grammar* and the *Practice Sentences*.

PRACTICE SENTENCES

These are substantial sentences illustrative of the work of a chapter; but they are not to be regarded as a substitute for the genuine Roman *Sententiae Antiquae* of each chapter in Wheelock's *Latin Grammar*.

No doubt a person would soon discover that some of the drill material and all the Practice Sentences have been selected from the Optional Self-Tutorial Exercises in Wheelock's *Latin Grammar*. There is a key for this material at the end of the book. However, as a matter of mature common sense and of one's own practical instruction, one should always write out these exercises for correction independently *before* ever consulting the key. Consulting the key first would obviously be a complete futility and waste of time. The fill-ins may be corrected in the classroom or photocopied to turn in to the instructor if required. Of course, if a person is using this *Workbook* with Wheelock's *Latin Grammar* as a private or self-paced study project, then the key (newly added to this edition) may ultimately provide the easiest method for correcting the answers.

My first debt of gratitude is owed to Professor Wheelock for granting permission to use some of his material in this form and for painstakingly reviewing and editing the two preliminary versions of this workbook. The wisdom of his advice and the perceptiveness of his comments have greatly contributed to improving the quality of the workbook. Without his encouragement and support, the project could not have been concluded. Ms. Nancy Cone, Editor of the Barnes and Noble Division of Harper & Row, deserves an expression of appreciation for her kind help in the publication of first edition of the workbook. I am also grateful to Professor Charles Elerick, Department of Linguistics, University of Texas at El Paso and Professor Jacques Laroche, Department of Foreign Languages, New Mexico State University, for having patiently worked with the two preliminary versions in their classrooms during the two-year period and for having made many helpful suggestions. I also acknowledge the helpfulness of many courageous students in my class sections from the Fall of 1976 to 1979 who struggled through the course while the material was being tested. I further express my thanks to the typists, Mrs. Bertha Nava and Mrs. Gloria Lewis, who transformed a difficult manuscript into a finished product of professional quality for the first edition. Any errors, inaccuracies or misconceptions are mine alone.

P.D.C.

Workbook for Wheelock's Latin Grammar

1

First and Second Conjugations; Present Infinitive, Indicative and Imperative Active

OBJECTIVES

1. To understand the difference between the factors which mark person and number of an English verb tense and those which mark a Latin verb tense.

2. To learn the active voice personal endings of a Latin verb.

3. To learn the present tense of the infinitive, and the indicative and imperative moods, active voice, of the Latin first and second conjugations.

GRAMMAR

(Memorize paradigms (models) and vocabulary by repeating them aloud!)

1. Person and number in an English tense are determined by the
_____.

2. Person and number in a Latin tense are determined by the
_____.

3. Write the personal endings for the active voice of a Latin verb and give the English pronoun equivalent to each.

Singular Latin Ending	English Pronoun(s)	Plural Latin Ending	English Pronoun(s)
1. _____ or = _____		1. _____ = _____	
2. _____ = _____		2. _____ = _____	
3. _____ = _____		3. _____ = _____	

4. The present active infinitive of the Latin verb which means *to praise* is _____(It will serve as the model verb for the first conjugation throughout the course.)

5. The present active infinitive of the Latin verb which means *to advise* is _____(It will serve as the model for the second conjugation throughout the course.)

6. The following forms are _____of Latin verbs. Give the conjugation to which they belong and their English meaning.

	Conjugation	Meaning(s)
a. vidēre	_____	_____
b. dare	_____	_____
c. valēre	_____	_____
d. cōgitāre	_____	_____
e. dēbēre	_____	_____
f. amāre	_____	_____
g. servāre	_____	_____
h. vocāre	_____	_____
i. cōnservāre	_____	_____
j. errāre	_____	_____

7. The present stem is formed by dropping _____from the _____which produces the stem_____for the first conjugation and _____for the second conjugation.

8. Write the conjugation of **dō** in the present indicative active and the three English present forms which translate it.

Latin	English Form 1	English Form 2	English Form 3
Singular			
1. _____	_____	_____	_____
2. _____	_____	_____	_____
3. _____	_____	_____	_____
Plural			
1. _____	_____	_____	_____
2. _____	_____	_____	_____
3. _____	_____	_____	_____

9. Write the conjugation of **dēbēo** in the present indicative active and the three English present forms which translate it.

Latin	English Form 1	English Form 2	English Porm 3
Singular			
1. _____	_____	_____	_____
2. _____	_____	_____	_____
3. _____	_____	_____	_____
Plural			
1. _____	_____	_____	_____
2. _____	_____	_____	_____
3. _____	_____	_____	_____

10. The model, pattern or example forms for the words of an inflected language are called _____

DRILL

Name _____ Section_____Date_____

A. Fill in the following blanks with the information requested.

	Person	Number	Tense	Mood	Voice	Translation
a. vocā	_____	_____	_____	_____	_____	_____
b. valēte	_____	_____	_____	_____	_____	_____
c. vidēte	_____	_____	_____	_____	_____	_____
d. dā	_____	_____	_____	_____	_____	_____
e. cōgitā	_____	_____	_____	_____	_____	_____
f. cōgitāte	_____	_____	_____	_____	_____	_____
g. valē	_____	_____	_____	_____	_____	_____
h. vidē	_____	_____	_____	_____	_____	_____
i. date	_____	_____	_____	_____	_____	_____
j. vocāte	_____	_____	_____	_____	_____	_____

B. Fill in the blanks for each verb:

	Person	Number	Tense	Mood	Voice	Translation
a. vocat	_____	_____	_____	_____	_____	_____
b. cōgitāmus	_____	_____	_____	_____	_____	_____
c. amant	_____	_____	_____	_____	_____	_____
d. dēbēs	_____	_____	_____	_____	_____	_____
e. videt	_____	_____	_____	_____	_____	_____
f. vident	_____	_____	_____	_____	_____	_____
g. dēbēmus	_____	_____	_____	_____	_____	_____
h. valēs	_____	_____	_____	_____	_____	_____
i. datis	_____	_____	_____	_____	_____	_____
j. amās	_____	_____	_____	_____	_____	_____

C. Supply the correct present active indicative form of the verb in parentheses and translate.

a. Saepe_____   (Errāre; 2nd person plural)

_____

b._____nihil .   (Vidēre; 1st person plural)

_____

c._____mē .   (Amāre; 3rd person singular)

_____

d. Quid_____?   (Vidēre; 2nd person plural)

_____

e. Vocā mē sī_____.   Errāre; 3rd person plural)

_____

f. _____nihil.   (Dare; 2nd person plural)

_____

g. Quid_____?   (Servāre; 1st person plural)

_____

h. Saepe nihil _____.   (Dare; 3rd person singular)

_____

i. Mē _____.   (Amāre; 3rd person plural)

_____

j. Monē mē sī nihil   .   (Vidēre; 2nd person singular)

_____

PRACTICE SENTENCES

(Before translating each, read the Latin <u>aloud</u> twice.)

a. Monent mē sī errō. _____

b. Monet mē sī errant. _____

c. Monēte mē sī errat. _____

d. Dēbēs monēre mē. _____

e. Dēbētis servāre mē. _____

f. Nōn dēbent laudāre mē. _____

g. "Quid dat?" "Saepe nihil dat." _____

h. Mē saepe vocant et (and) monent. _____

i. Nihil videō. Quid vidēs? _____

j. Mē laudā sī nōn errō. _____

k. Sī valētis, valēmus. _____

l. Sī valet, valeō. _____

m. Sī mē amat, dēbet mē laudāre. _____

n. Cōnservāte mē. _____

o. Nōn dēbe errāre. _____

p. Quid dēbēmus laudāre? _____

q. Videt; cōgitat; monet. _____

2

Cases: First Declension; Agreement of Adjectives

OBJECTIVES

1. To learn each case or form of a Latin noun and the role or function or use of each one in a Latin sentence.

2. To learn the declension and gender of first declension nouns and adjectives.

GRAMMAR

(Memorize paradigms (models) and vocabulary by repeating them aloud!)

1. The Latin expressions for the definite article "the" and the indefinite articles "a" or "an" are _____.

2. Name the Latin cases representing each of the following constructions or ideas:

a. Direct object of a verb _____

b. Possession _____

c. Subject of a verb _____

d. Means _____

e. Direct address _____

f. Agent _____

g. Indirect object of a verb _____

h. Manner _____

i. Accompaniment _____

j. Place _____

3. Fill in the following blanks with the information requested for each first declension ending.

	Case	Number	Function	English Preposition(s) (if any)
-ās	_____	_____	_____	_____
-a	vocative	_____	_____	_____
-am	vocative	_____	_____	_____
-ae	dative	_____	_____	_____
-a	nominative	_____	_____	_____
-ā	_____	_____	_____	_____
-īs	ablative	_____	_____	_____
-ae	genitive	_____	_____	_____
-ae	nominative	_____	_____	_____
-īs	dative	_____	_____	_____
-ārum	_____	_____	_____	_____

4. Though Latin first declension nouns are normally feminine, three examples of masculine nouns of that declension are:

Latin   **English**

_____   _____

_____   _____

_____   _____

5. Complete the declension:

Singular	**Case**	**English Meaning(s)**
_____Pecūnia_____	_____	_____
_____	_____	_____
_____	_____	_____
_____	_____	_____
_____	_____	_____
_____	_____	_____

Plural	Case	English Meaning(s)
____Pecūniae_____	_____	_____
_____	_____	_____
_____	_____	_____
_____	_____	_____
_____	_____	_____
_____	_____	_____

6. Fill in the following blanks with the information requested for each noun.

	English Meaning	Use & English Preposition(s) (if any)
a. fōrmam	_____	_____
b. fāma	_____	_____
c. fortūnās	_____	_____
d. īrae (nominative plural)	_____	_____
e. philosophiae (dative singular)	_____	_____
f. puellīs	_____	_____
g. pecūnia	_____	_____
h. vītae (genitive singular)	_____	_____
i. poenārum	_____	_____
j. patriīs	_____	_____

DRILL

Name_____ **Section**_____ **Date**_____

Supply the correct form of the words, shown in parentheses in the nominative case, and translate:

a. _____(puella) cōgitat.

_____

b. Date _____(pecūnia).

_____

c. Sine _____(īra) monet.

_____

d. Vidēmus _____(fōrma; plural).

_____

e. _____(nauta) dant _____(poena; plural).

_____

f. Amātis _____(vīta; singular) et _____(puella; plural).

_____

g. Est sine _____(multa pecūnia; singular).

_____

h. Nōn servās _____(patria).

_____

i. _____(fortūna) vocat.

_____

j. Laudō _____(philosophia antīqua).

_____

k. Cōnservant tuam philosophiam _____(vīta; genitive).

_____

l. Fōrma _____(porta, genitive plural) est antīqua.

_____

PRACTICE SENTENCES

(Before translating each, read the Latin <u>aloud</u> twice.)

a. Valē, patria mea. _____

b. Fortūna puellae est magna. _____

c. Puella fortūnam patriae tuae laudat. _____

_____

d. Ō puella, patriam tuam servā._____

e. Multae puellae pecūniam amant. _____

f. Puellae nihil datis._____

g. Pecūniam puellae videt. _____

h. Pecūniam puellārum nōn vidēs. _____

_____

i. Monēre puellās dēbēmus._____

j. Laudāre puellam dēbent. _____

k. Vīta multīs puellīs fortūnam dat. _____

l. Vītam meam pecūniā tuā cōnservās._____

_____

m. Fāma est nihil sine fortūnā ._____

n. Vītam sine pecūniā nōn amātis. _____

_____

o. Sine famā et fortūnā patria nōn valet. _____

_____

p. Iram puellārum laudāre nōn dēbēs._____

_____

q. Vītam sine poenīs amāmus. _____

r. Sine philosophiā nōn valēmus. _____

s. Quid est vīta sine philosophiā ? _____

3

Second Declension: Masculine Nouns and Adjectives; Word Order

OBJECTIVES

1. To know and understand the implications of the usual order of words in the English sentence and in a Latin sentence.

2. To learn the declension of second declension masculine nouns ending in -us and -er and second declension masculine adjectives ending in -us.

GRAMMAR

(Memorize paradigms (models) and vocabulary by repeating them aloud!)

1. In English, the order of words in a sentence is (Circle one.)

   crucial   secondary

2. In Latin, the order of words in a sentence is (Circle one.)
   crucial   secondary

3. Assign numbers 1-5 to the following to show the typical order of words in a simple Latin sentence or clause:

_____ Subject and its modifiers

_____ Verb

_____ Adverbial words or phrases

_____ Direct object

_____ Indirect object

4. The typical order listed above reflects the Roman fondness for a style indicating (Circle one.)

                emphasis   suspense   variety

5. Nouns of the second declension with nominatives ending in **-us** or **-er** are generally (Circle one.)

                masculine   feminine   neuter

6. Give the indicated information for each of the following second declension masculine case endings.

Case	Number	Function	English Preposition(s) (if any)
-ō ablative			
-um			
-ō dative			
-ī vocative			
-ōrum			
-us			
-ōs			
-ī (sing)			
-e			
-īs ablative			
-ī nominative			
-īs dative			

7. Give the indicated information for each of the following:

	Case	Function	Translation
a. fīliōrum meōrum	ablative		
b. fīliō meō	genitive		
c. populī Rōmānī	dative		
d. populō Rōmānō	ablative		
e. virīs Rōmānīs	nominative		
f. virī magnī			
g. virōrum Rōmānōrum			
h. amīcōrum paucōrum			
i. amīcīs meī e	dative		
j. amīcō meō	ablative		
k. amīcī Rōmānī	vocative		
l. multīs puerīs	ablative		
m. magnum virum			
n. puer meus			
o. multōs agrōs			
p. magnī numerī (sing)			
q. numerī meī	nominative		
r. puerōrum meōrum			
s. populus Rōmānus			
t. amīce magne			

DRILL

Name_____ Section_____Date_____

A. Supply the correct form of the words, shown in parentheses in the nominative case, and translate:

a. Habēmus semper _____(sapientia).

_____

b. Numerus (puer; genitive plural) errat. _____

_____

c. Dat sapientiam (fīlius meus; dative plural). _____

_____

d. Paucī puerī vident _____(numerus magnus; singular)

_____(vir magnus; genitive plural).

_____

e. Vocāte _____(vir; plural)_____ (magna sapientia; genitive singular). _____

_____

B. Translate the following:

a. The wisdom of men is great.

_____

b. The people give much money to the sons of Romans.

_____

c. My son sees the girl.

_____

d. We praise the boy's friends.

_____

e. Many men do not love the great wisdom of philosophy.

_____

PRACTICE SENTENCES

(Before translating each, read the Latin <u>aloud</u> twice.)

a. Valē, mī amīce. _____

b. Populus Rōmānus sapientiam fīliī tuī laudat. _____
_____

c. Ō vir magne, populum Rōmānum servā.
_____
_____

d. Numerus populī Rōmānī est magnus. _____
_____

e. Multī puerī puellās amant. _____

f. Fīliō meō nihil datis. _____

g. Virōs in agrō videō. _____

h. Amīcum fīliī meī vidēs. _____

i. Amīcum fīliōrum tuōrum nōn videt. _____
_____

j. Dēbēmus fīliōs meōs monēre. _____

k. Dēbent fīlium tuum laudāre. _____

l. Vīta paucīs virīs fāmam dat. _____

m. Mē in numerō amīcōrum tuōrum habēs. _____
_____

n. Virī magnī paucōs amīcōs saepe habent. _____
_____

o. Amīcus meus semper cōgitat. _____

p. Fīlius magnī virī nōn semper est magnus vir. _____
_____

q. Sapientiam magnōrum virōrum nōn semper vidēmus . _____
_____

r. Philosophiam, sapientiam magnōrum virōrum, laudāre dēbētis. _____
_____

4

Second Declension: Neuters; Summary of Adjectives; Present of Sum; Predicate Nouns and Adjectives

OBJECTIVES

1. To learn the declension of neuter nouns and adjectives of the second declension.

2. To review the complete declension of first/second declension adjectives ending in -us, -a, -um (masculine, feminine, neuter).

3. To learn the conjugation of the irregular verb esse (to be) in the present indicative tense.

4. To learn the function of predicate nouns and adjectives in Latin syntax.

GRAMMAR

(Memorize paradigms (models) and vocabulary by repeating them aloud!)

1. Except in the nominative, accusative and vocative cases, the forms or inflections of the neuter second declension nouns are the same as (Circle one.)

Declension 1 masculine   Declension 2 masculine   Declension 1 feminine

2. The first declension contains no nouns of which of the following genders? (Circle one.)

Masculine   Feminine   Neuter

3. The two cases which always have the same ending in the neuter gender only are (Circle one.)

Dative & ablative   Nominative & accusative   Nominative & genitive

4. Fill in the following blanks with the information requested for each second declension neuter ending:

Case	Number	Function	English Preposition(s) (if any)
-ōrum _____	_____	_____	_____
-ī _____	_____	_____	_____
-um accusative	_____	_____	_____

Case	Number	Function	English Preposition(s) (if any)
-īs ablative	_____	_____	_____
-ō ablative	_____	_____	_____
-um nominative	_____	_____	_____
-a accusative	_____	_____	_____
-īs dative	_____	_____	_____
-ō dative	_____	_____	_____
-a nominative	_____	_____	_____

5. Adjectives have masculine, feminine and neuter endings so that, in addition to agreeing in number and case, they may agree in

_____ .

6. Complete the declension (omit the vocative).

		Case	English Meaning(s)
officium	vērum		

7. Fill in the following blanks with the information requested for each noun.

	Translation	Function
a. donōrum		
b. cōnsiliī		
c. officiō		
d. perīculīs		
e. bella		

8. The personal endings of **esse** in the present indicative, when compared with the standard active voice personal endings in Latin, are (Circle one.)

      identical   different

9. Since **esse** is an intransitive verb, it serves to connect a subject with another noun or adjective called a (Circle one.)

      direct object   predicate

10. Predicate nouns must always **agree** with their subject in case and number but not always in.

11. Translate the following:

    a. sumus _____

    b. sunt _____

    c. sum _____

    d. estis _____

    e. est _____

    f. es _____

DRILL

Name _____ **Section**_____**Date**_____

A. Translate each of the following into Latin or English.

a. real danger (subject) _____

b. ōtium magnum _____

c. bella mala _____

d. dōna bella _____

e. from a foolish plan _____

f. perīculī vērī _____

g. for great leisure _____

h. an evil war (direct object) _____

i. by beautiful gifts _____

j. cōnsilia stulta _____

k. of small services _____

l. officiō parvō _____

B. Supply the correct forms of the words shown in parentheses in the nominative case and translate.

a. _____(perīculum) sunt _____(vērus, a, um).

_____

b. Perīculum _____(bellum, genitive) _____est

(parvus, a, um)._____

c. Puer et puella sunt _____(bellus, a, um).

_____

d. Officium et ōtium sunt _____(bonus, a, um).

_____

e. Video _____(cūra; plural) et _____(mora;

plural). _____

C. Translate the following:

a. War is evil.

_____

b. Peace is good.

_____

c. The teacher loves service.

_____

d. Your eyes are pretty.

_____

e. The danger of delays is real.

_____

PRACTICE SENTENCES

(Before translating each, read the Latin aloud twice.)

a. Multa bella ōtium nōn cōnservant. _____

_____

b. Et ōtium perīcula saepe habet. _____

_____

c. Stultus vir perīcula bellī laudat. _____

_____

d. Ōtium bellō saepe nōn cōnservāmus. _____

_____

e. Populus Rōmānus ōtium bonum nōn semper habet. _____

_____

f. Patriam et ōtium bellīs parvīs saepe servant. _____

_____

g. Sine morā cūram officiō dare dēbēmus. _____

_____

h. Perīculum est magnum. _____

i. In magnō perīculō sumus. _____

_____

j. Vīta nōn est sine multīs perīculīs. _____

_____

k. Amīcus meus est vir magnī officiī. _____

_____

l. Officia magistrī sunt multa et magna. _____

_____

m. Vir parvī ōtiī es. _____

n. Virī magnae cūrae estis. _____

o. Sine oculīs vīta est nihil. _____

_____

5

First and Second Conjugations: Future Indicative Active; Adjectives of the First and Second Declension in -er

OBJECTIVES

1. To learn the conjugation of the active future indicative of the Latin first and second conjugations.

2. To learn the declension of the first and second declension adjectives ending in -er.

GRAMMAR

(Memorize paradigms (models) and vocabulary by repeating them aloud!)

1. The present stems for the first two conjugations studied in Chapter 1 were obtained by dropping _____ from **laudāre** and _____ from **monēre** to produce the stems _____ and _____

2. The active indicative future used to indicate future time in the Latin first and second conjugations is composed of three elements in the following order: _____, _____ and _____.

3. Give the **personal endings** only for the following active indicative tenses of the first two conjugations:

Present		Future	
Singular	Plural	Singular	Plural
1._____	_____	1._____	_____
2._____	_____	2._____	_____
3._____	_____	3._____	_____

4. Give the **future tense sign** only for the first two conjugations:

First		Second	
Singular	Plural	Singular	Plural
1._____	_____	1._____	_____
2._____	_____	2._____	_____
3._____	_____	3._____	_____

5. Write the conjugation of the active indicative future in Latin and English of the following:

Vocāre	To call	Habēre	To have
Singular			
1._____	_____	_____	_____
2._____	_____	_____	_____
3._____	_____	_____	_____
Plural			
1._____	_____	_____	_____
2._____	_____	_____	_____
3._____	_____	_____	_____

6. When we studied second declension Latin nouns ending in **-er** like **ager** and **puer,** we discovered that the only way to tell whether the **e** remained or was dropped was to memorize the genitive form; and we also discovered that the genitive provides the stem for the other cases, i.e., **agrī** and **puerī**. Adjectives of Declension 1/2 with a masculine **-er** ending include some which retain and some which drop the **e**. What forms of these adjectives must be memorized to detect the stem for the other cases?

_____   _____   _____   _____

7. Decline the following adjectives:

Singular

Nom	līber	lībera	līberum	noster	nostra	nostrum
Gen	_____	_____	_____	_____	_____	_____
Dat	_____	_____	_____	_____	_____	_____
Acc	_____	_____	_____	_____	_____	_____
Abl	_____	_____	_____	_____	_____	_____

Plural

Nom	_____	_____	_____	_____	_____	_____
Gen	_____	_____	_____	_____	_____	_____
Dat	_____	_____	_____	_____	_____	_____
Acc	_____	_____	_____	_____	_____	_____
Abl	_____	_____	_____	_____	_____	_____

DRILL

Name _____ Section_____Date_____

A. Translate the following into English or Latin.

     a. amābimus   _____

     b. valēbit   _____

     c. vidēbunt   _____

     d. superābimus   _____

     e. cogitābō   _____

     f. I shall have   _____

     g. You (plural) will have _____

     h. She will err   _____

     i. We shall give   _____

     j. They will remain   _____

B. Supply the correct forms of the words shown in parentheses and translate.

     a. Animī (plural) _____ (superāre; future).
_____

     b. _____(superāre, 1st person plural, future) perīcula.
_____

     c. Sapientia satis _____ (valēre; future).
_____

     d. _____(dare, 2nd Person plural, future) glōriam amīcō.
_____

     e. Tum culpa nostra _____ (remanēre; future).
_____

     f. Puella et puer _____ (errāre; future).
_____

     g. _____ (vidēre, 1st person singular, future) magistrōs.
_____

     h. Morae et cūrae _____ (remanēre; future).
_____

     i. _____ (cōgitāre, 2nd person singular, future) dē
     philosophiā._____

     j. Propter bellum igitur tē _____ (superāre, 1st per-
     son singular, future)._____

PRACTICE SENTENCES

(Before translating each, read the Latin <u>aloud</u> twice.)

a. Magister noster mē laudat et tē laudābit. _____

_____

b. Līberī virī perīcula nostra superābunt. _____

_____

c. Fīliī nostrī puellās pulchrās amant. _____

_____

d. Culpās multās habēmus et semper habēbimus. _____

_____

e. Pulchra patria nostra est lībera. _____

_____

f. Līberī virī estis; patriam pulchram habēbitis. _____

_____

g. Magistrī līberī officiō cūram dabunt. _____

_____

h. Sī īram tuam superābis, tē superābis. _____

_____

i. Propter nostrōs animōs multī sunt līberī. _____

_____

j. Habetne animus tuus satis sapientiae? _____

_____

6

Sum: Future and Imperfect Indicative; Possum: Complementary Infinitive

OBJECTIVES

*1. To learn the active indicative future and imperfect of **esse**.*
*2. To learn the active indicative present, future and imperfect of **posse**.*
3. To know the syntax governing complementary infinitives.

GRAMMAR

(Memorize paradigms (models) and vocabulary by repeating them aloud!)

1. In order to say "**to be able**," the Romans originally combined the root **pot (potis**, able) with esse to produce potesse which later became _____ = **to be able, can.**

2. **Posse**, like **dēbēre**, is regularly followed by an infinitive whose function is to _____ the meaning of **posse.**

3. A complementary infinitive (Circle one.)

      has its own subject   uses that of **dēbēre** or **posse**

4. Conjugate **esse** in the active indicative tenses indicated:

	Present		**Future**		**Imperfect**	
	Latin	English	Latin	English	Latin	English
Singular						
1.	_____	_____	_____	_____	_____	_____
2.	_____	_____	_____	_____	_____	_____
3.	_____	_____	_____	_____	_____	_____
Plural						
1.	_____	_____	_____	_____	_____	_____
2.	_____	_____	_____	_____	_____	_____
3.	_____	_____	_____	_____	_____	_____

5. Conjugate **posse** in the active tenses indicated:

	Present		**Future**		**Imperfect**	
	Latin	English	Latin	English	Latin	English
Singular						
1.	_____	_____	_____	_____	_____	_____
2.	_____	_____	_____	_____	_____	_____
3.	_____	_____	_____	_____	_____	_____
Plural						
1.	_____	_____	_____	_____	_____	_____
2.	_____	_____	_____	_____	_____	_____
3.	_____	_____	_____	_____	_____	_____

DRILL

Name _____ **Section** _____ **Date** _____

A. Translate the following into English or Latin.

a. erat _____

b. poterit _____

c. poterāmus _____

d. erō _____

e. poterunt _____

f. we shall be able to _____

g. I can _____

h. you were able to _____

i. he will be _____

j. we were _____

B. Supply the correct forms of the words shown in parentheses and translate:

a. Librī Graecōrum _____ (esse; imperfect) vērī.

_____

b. Liber vester _____(esse; future) vērus.

_____

c. Librī nostrī _____(esse; present) vērī.

_____

d. Nōn _____ (posse; 1st person plural; imperfect) tolerāre vitia tyrannōrum. _____

_____

e. Nōn _____ (posse, 1st person plural, future) tolerāre librōs malos. _____

f. Nōn _____ (posse, 1st person plural, present) tolerāre vestrās culpās. _____

g. Ubi _____ (posse, 2nd person singular, imperfect) superāre tyrannōs? Ibi. _____

h. Ubi _____ (posse, 2nd person singular, present) superāre īnsidiās tyrannōrum? Ibi. _____

i. Ubi _____ (posse, 2nd person singular, future) superāre insidiās nostrās? Ibi. _____

_____

j. Insidiae Graecōrum _____ (esse, imperfect) perpetuae.

_____

PRACTICE SENTENCES

(Before translating each, read the Latin <u>aloud</u> twice.)

a. Patria vestra erat lībera. _____

_____

b. Amīcus vester erit tyrannus. _____

_____

c. Ubi tyrannus est, virī nōn possunt esse līberī. _____

_____

d. Tyrannī multa vitia semper habēbunt. _____

_____

e. Tyrannum nostrum superāre dēbēmus. _____

_____

f. Poteritis perīcula tyrannī vidēre. _____

_____

g. Īnsidiās tyrannī nōn tolerābis. _____

_____

h. Dēbēs virōs līberōs dē tyrannīs monēre. _____

_____

i. Librī bonī vērīque poterant patriam cōnservāre. _____

_____

j. Tyrannī sapientiam bonōrum librōrum superāre nōn poterunt. _____

_____

_____

7

Third Declension: Nouns

OBJECTIVE

To learn the declension of the third declension consonant-stem nouns in the masculine, feminine and neuter genders.

GRAMMAR

(Memorize paradigms (models) and vocabulary by repeating them aloud!)

1. Gender presents a great difficulty in the 3rd declension because that declension includes a variety of all genders. The safest procedure is to memorize the gender. One of the declension's features, however, is that nouns denoting human beings are _____ or _____ according to meaning.

2. In the 3rd declension, the gender of nouns (can, cannot) ordinarily be identified by the endings as was the case with 1st and 2nd declension nouns.

3. Give the information requested below for each of the third declension endings listed.

	Case(s)	Number	Gender(s)
1. -um	_____	_____	_____
2. -ibus	_____	_____	_____
3. -a	_____	_____	_____
4. -ēs	_____	_____	_____
5. -is	_____	_____	_____
6. -em	_____	_____	_____
7. -e	_____	_____	_____
8. -ī	_____	_____	_____

4. Give the proper nominative singular form of the adjective **magnus, a, um** to accompany the following 3rd declension nouns:

a. tempus	_____	f. pāx	_____
b. virtūs	_____	g. rēx	_____
c. labor	_____	h. corpus	_____
d. cīvitās	_____	i. virgō	_____
e. mōs	_____	j. amor	_____

DRILL

Name _____ Section_____Date _____

A. Translate the following into English or Latin.

a. laborēs multi _____

b. pācis perpetuae _____

c. cīvitātum parvārum _____

d. cīvitāte parvā _____

e. tempora mala _____

f. great virtues (dir. obj.) _____

g. with great courage _____

h. our times (subj.) _____

i. to/for our times _____

j. by my love _____

B. Supply the correct forms of the words shown in parentheses and translate.

a. Audēbimus servāre _____ (pāx).

_____

b. _____ (mōrēs) _____ (homō, genitive plural)

sunt malī. _____

c. Propter _____ (virtus), audēbimus ibi remanēre.

_____

d. In _____ (labor) est _____ (virtūs).

_____

e. Nōn habēbitis satis _____ (tempus).

_____

f. Sine _____ (litterae), nōn possumus servāre _____

(amor) _____

g. Graecae _____ (virgō) erant bellae.

_____

h. Nōn habēmus _____ (pāx) in _____ (cīvitās,

plural). _____

i. Mōs _____ (labor, genitive) semper dabit _____

(mōrēs) (homō, plural).

_____

j. Poterisne superāre sine _____ (virtūs)?

_____

PRACTICE SENTENCES

(Before translating each, read the Latin <u>aloud</u> twice.)

a. Pecūnia est nihil sine mōribus bonīs. _____

_____

b. Mōrēs hominis bonī erunt bonī. _____

_____

c. Hominī litterās dabunt. _____

_____

d. Magnum amōrem pecūniae in multīs hominibus vidēmus. _____

_____

e. Cīvitās nostra pēcem hominibus multīs dabit. _____

_____

f. Sine bonā pāce cīvitātēs temporum nostrōrum nōn valēbunt _____

_____

g. In multīs cīvitātibus terrīsque pāx nōn poterat valēre. _____

_____

h. Virgō pulchra amīcōs mōrum bonōrum amat. _____

_____

i. Hominēs magnae virtūtis tyrannōs superāre audēbunt. _____

_____

j. Amos patriae in cīvitāte nostrā valet. _____

_____

8

Third Conjugation: Present Infinitive, Present and Future Indicative, Present Imperative Active

OBJECTIVE

To learn the conjugation of the active infinitive present, the indicative present and future and the imperative present of the Latin third conjugation verbs.

GRAMMAR

(Memorize paradigms (models) and vocabulary by repeating them aloud!)

1. What vowels appear in the endings of the active indicative present in the third conjugation?

   _____   _____   _____

2. What vowels appear in the endings of the active indicative future in the third conjugation?

   _____   _____   _____

3. Give the active imperative present for the verbs **dūcere, dīcere, facere, ferre, mittere** and **pōnere:**

	dūcere	**dīcere**	**facere**
2nd Sing.	_____	_____	_____
2nd Plur.	_____	_____	_____

	ferre	**mittere**	**pōnere:**
2nd Sing.	_____	_____	_____
2nd Plur.	_____	_____	_____

4. Give information requested for each of the following endings:

	Tense	**Number**	**Person**
a. -imus	_____	_____	_____
b. -es	_____	_____	_____
c. -unt	_____	_____	_____
d. -et	_____	_____	_____
e. -itis	_____	_____	_____

	Tense	**Number**	**Person**
f. -ēmus	_____	_____	_____
g -ō	_____	_____	_____
h. -ent	_____	_____	_____
i. -it	_____	_____	_____
j. -ētis	_____	_____	_____
k. -is	_____	_____	_____
i. -am	_____	_____	_____

DRILL

Name _____ **Section** _____ **Date** _____

A. Given the verbs **mittere**, to send, **agere**, to do, **scrībere**, to write, **pōnere**, to put, translate the following into English or Latin.

a. mittent _____   m. they are putting _____

b. mittunt _____   n. we shall put _____

c. mitte _____   o. put (imp. sing.) _____

d. mittimus _____   p. he puts _____

e. mittētis _____   q. they will put _____

f. agit _____   r. I shall put _____

g. agam _____   s. you (sing.) are putting _____

h. agēmu _____   t. you (plu.) will put _____

i. agis _____   u. put (imp. plu.) _____

j. scrībet _____   v. we put _____

k. scrībite _____   w. you (plu.) are putting _____

l. scrībitis _____   x. he will put _____

B. Supply the correct forms of the words shown in parentheses and translate.

a. Ratiō _____ (agere; present) hominēs.

_____

b. _____(scrībere; 2nd person singular, imperative) nihil dē cōpiīs.

_____

c. Post bellum, _____ (mittere; 1st person singular, future) litterās.

_____

d. _____ (mittere; 3rd person singular, present) cōpiam librōrum.

_____

e. Grātiās _____ (agere; 2nd person plural, future) amīcō vestrō.

_____

C. Translate the following:

a. Dare to tolerate good judgment. _____

_____

b. He will lead the troops to (toward) glory. _____

_____

c. The state will thank the tyrant. _____

_____

d. Your (sing) friend is sending a letter. _____

_____

e. Because of your work, you will have an abundance of money. _____

_____

PRACTICE SENTENCES

(Before translating each, read the Latin <u>aloud</u> twice.)

a. Hominem ad mē dūcunt. _____

_____

b. Dūc hominem ad mē, et hominī grātiās agam. _____

_____

c. Dum tyrannus cōpiās dūcit, possumus nihil agere. _____

_____

d. Librōs dē pāce scrībēmus. _____

_____

e. Puerī magistrō grātiās nōn agunt. _____

_____

f. Paucī cīvitātī nostrae grātiās agent. _____

_____

g. Tyrannus magnās cōpiās ex cīvitāte nostrā dūcet. _____

_____

h. Magna cōpia pecūniae hominēs ad sapientiam nōn dūcit. ___

_____

i. Dūcimusne saepe hominēs ad ratiōnem? _____

_____

j. Ratiō hominēs ad bonam vītam dūcere potest. _____

_____

9

Demonstrative Pronouns: Hic, Ille, Iste

OBJECTIVES

*1. To learn the declension and use of the Latin demonstratives **hic, ille** and **iste**.*

2. To observe carefully the peculiar forms of the genitive and dative singular.

3. To note that demonstratives can be used as adjectives or pronouns.

*4. To learn the peculiar declension of certain first and second declension adjectives which have **-ius** in the genitive singular and **-ī** in the dative singular.*

GRAMMAR

(Memorize paradigms and vocabulary by repeating them aloud!)

1. Adjectives/pronouns used by the Romans to _____ persons or things are called _____.

2. The declension difficulties of the Latin demonstratives come chiefly from the irregularity of three singular cases. They are:

   _____ _____ _____

3. For all practical purposes, Latin demonstratives are declined like adjectives of the _____declension and therefore like paradigm _____.

4. Give the information requested below for each of the Latin adjectives/ pronouns listed.

	Case(s)	Number(s)	Gender(s)	Translation(s)
a. istud				
b. istī				
c. istīs				
d. istīus				
e. istō				
f. illārum				
g. illī				
h. ille				
i. illa				
j. illum				
k. haec				
l. huius				
m. hoc				
n. huic				
o. hunc				
p. hōrum				
q. iste				
r. hōs				
s. illam				
t. illae				

6. Give the information requested below for each of the following Latin irregular adjectives of the first and second declensions.

	Case(s)	Number(s)	Gender(s)	Translation(s)
a. ullīus				
b. nūllīus				
c. nūllam				
d. ūllō				
e. tōtō				
f. tōtīus				
g. tōtī				
h. sōlō				
i. sōlī				
j. sōlum				
k. ūnīus				
l. ūnum				
m. ūnī				
n. alterīus				
o. aliī				
p. aliā				
q. aliud				
r. alterī				
s. aliōrum				
t. alterum				

DRILL

Name _____ **Section**_____**Date**_____

A. Translate the following into English or Latin.

a. haec puella _____

b. illa puella _____

c. huic temporī _____

d. huius temporis _____

e. illī puerō _____

f. nūllī librō _____

g. huic cīvitātī sōlī _____

h. tōtīus patriae _____

i. nūllīus ratiōnis _____

j. huius cīvitātis sōlīus _____

k. no reason (acc.) _____

l. to/for the whole country _____

m. to/for one city _____

n. no books (acc.) _____

o. by another book _____

p. to/for that boy alone _____

q. those times (acc.) _____

r. that time (nom.) _____

s. of that girl alone _____

t. to/for one girl _____

B. Supply the correct form of the words shown in parentheses and translate.

a. _____ (tōtus, -a, -um) locus erat vērus.

_____

b. Habētis _____ (nūllus, -a, -um) vitia.

_____

c. Vidēbimus _____ (sōlus, -a, -um) bona loca.

_____

d. Fāma _____ (iste, -a, -ud) locī remanet.

_____

e. Multī locī _____ (hic, haec, hoc) librī errant.

_____

C. Translate the following:

a. No passage of this letter is true.

_____

b. Another friend will thank my son.

_____

c. Lead your troops into that region.

_____

d. Without any reason, they will call.

_____

e. Your eyes will see those places.

_____

PRACTICE SENTENCES

(Before translating each, read the Latin <u>aloud</u> twice.)

a. Hī tōtam cīvitātem dūcent (dūcunt).

_____

b. In illō librō illa dē hōc homine scrībet (scrībam).

_____

c. Ūnus vir istās cōpiās in hanc terram dūcit (dūcet).

_____

d. Hunc librum dē aliō bellō scrībimus (scrībēmus).

_____

e. Tōta patria huic sōlī grātiās agit (aget).

_____

f. Hic vir sōlus mē dē vitiīs huius tyrannī monēre poterat.

_____

g. Nūllās cōpiās in alterā terrā habētis.

_____

h. Illī sōlī nūlla perīcula in hōc consiliō vident.

_____

i. Non sōlum mōrēs sed etiam īnsidiās illīus laudāre audēs.

_____

j. Propter īnsidiās enim ūnīus hominis haec cīvitās nōn valet.

_____

10

Fourth Conjugation and Verbs of the Third

OBJECTIVE

To learn the active infinitive present, the active indicative present and future, and the active imperative present of Latin verbs of the fourth conjugation (audiō, audīre) and -iō verbs of the third conjugation (capiō, capere).

GRAMMAR

(Memorize paradigms and vocabulary by repeating them aloud!)

1. Give the information requested for the infinitives presented on the following page:

	Conjugation	Meaning(s)
a. vīvere	_____	_____
b. invenīre	_____	_____
c. valēre	_____	_____
d. vocāre	_____	_____
e. vidēre	_____	_____
f. fugere	_____	_____
g. venīre	_____	_____
h. facere	_____	_____
i. servāre	_____	_____
j. capere	_____	_____
k. errāre	_____	_____
l. scrībere	_____	_____
m. docēre	_____	_____
n. audīre	_____	_____
o. dūcere	_____	_____
p. agere	_____	_____
q. audēre	_____	_____
r. tolerāre	_____	_____
s. remanēre	_____	_____
t. habēre	_____	_____

2. Complete the conjugation of the following and give the English meaning of each person:

Singular
1. vīvō _____ **fugiō** _____ **veniō** _____

2. _____ _____ _____ _____ _____ _____

3. _____ _____ _____ _____ _____ _____

Plural
1. _____ _____ _____ _____ _____ _____

2. _____ _____ _____ _____ _____ _____

3. _____ _____ _____ _____ _____ _____

3. Complete the conjugation of the following and give the Latin meaning for each person:

Singular
1. I shall act_____ **I shall make** _____ **I shall find** _____

2. _____ _____ _____ _____ _____ _____

3. _____ _____ _____ _____ _____ _____

Plural
1. _____ _____ _____ _____ _____ _____

2. _____ _____ _____ _____ _____ _____

3. _____ _____ _____ _____ _____ _____

4. Give the Latin imperative for the following:

Singular
Write _____ Live _____ Hear _____

Plural
Write _____ Live _____ Hear _____

DRILL

Name _____ Section _____ Date _____

A. Translate the following into English or Latin.

a. scrībe_____   k. I shall lead _____

b. fugimus_____   l. She will get _____

c. inveniētis _____   m. We shall hear _____

d. vīvent _____   n. You will do (plu.) _____

e. facis _____   o. I am making _____

f. venīmus _____   p. It is coming _____

g. agitis _____   q. We live _____

h. capiunt _____   r. You are fleeing (plu.) _____

i. audīte_____   s. Find (imper. sing.) _____

j. dūc_____   t. Write (imper. plur. _____

B. Supply the correct form of the words shown in parentheses and translate:

a. Tempus _____ (fugere, present).

_____

b. _____ (vīvere; 1st person plural; future) semper in pāce.

_____

c. Sapientia senectūtis _____ (invenīre, future) pācem.

_____

d. Nātūra _____ (invenīre; future) viam.

_____

e. Cum fīliā nostrā, _____ (fugere, 3rd person plural,

present) ad viam. _____

C. Translate the following:

a. Love will find you.

_____

b. The hour is fleeing.

_____

c. They come to see you often.

_____

d. Our daughter finds peace in nature.

_____

e. You will make a good road.

_____

PRACTICE SENTENCES

(Before translating each, read the Latin <u>aloud</u> twice.)

a. Cum fīliā tuā fuge. _____

_____

b. Tempus fugit; hōrae fugiunt; senectūs venit. _____

_____

c. In patriam vestram veniunt. _____

_____

d. Fīliam tuam in illā cīvitāte veniēs. _____

_____

e. Tyrannus viam in hanc cīvitātem invenit. _____

_____

f. Ad tē cum magnīs cōpiīs venīmus. _____

_____

g. Iste bellum semper facit. _____

_____

h. Multī hominēs illa faciunt sed haec nōn faciunt. _____

_____

i. Magnam cōpiam librōrum faciam. _____

_____

j. In librīs virōrum antīquōrum multam philosophiam et sapientiam in-
veniētis._____

_____

11

Personal Pronouns and Demonstrative Pronouns

OBJECTIVES

1. To learn to decline and to use the first and second person personal pronouns in the singular and the plural.

2. To learn to decline and to use the colorless or relatively weak Latin demonstrative **is, ea, id** which serves as the third person personal pronoun, and its derivative **īdem, eadem, idem**.

GRAMMAR

(Memorize paradigms and vocabulary by repeating them aloud!)

1. How many genders does the declension of the Latin first and second person personal pronouns include? (Circle one.)

   one   two   three

2. How many genders does the declension of the Latin third person personal pronouns include? (Circle one.)

   one   two   three

3. The nominatives of the Latin personal pronouns were: (Circle one.)

(a) not used by the Romans except for stress
(b) never expressed because they were dictated by the verb ending

4. The pronouns **nostrum** and **vestrum** were used by the Romans as (Circle one.)

possessive genitives   partitive genitives   objective genitives

5. The pronouns **nostrī** and **vestrī** were used by the Romans as (Circle one.)

possessive genitives   partitive genitives   objective genitives

6. Decline below the first and second person personal pronouns in the singular and plural and give the translations.

	1st Person		**2nd Person**	
Latin	**English Meaning(s)**	**Latin**	**English Meaning(s)**	
Singular				
Nom _____	_____	_____	_____	
Gen _____	_____	_____	_____	
Dat _____	_____	_____	_____	
Acc _____	_____	_____	_____	
Abl _____	_____	_____	_____	
Plural				
Nom _____	_____	_____	_____	
Gen _____	_____	_____	_____	
Dat _____	_____	_____	_____	
Acc _____	_____	_____	_____	
Abl _____	_____	_____	_____	

7. Decline below the third personal (demonstrative) pronoun in the singular and plural and give the translations.

Masculine		Feminine		Neuter	
Latin	English Meaning(s)	Latin	English Meaning(s)	Latin	English Meaning(s)
Singular					
Nom_____	_____	_____	_____	_____	_____
Gen_____	_____	_____	_____	_____	_____
Dat_____	_____	_____	_____	_____	_____
Acc_____	_____	_____	_____	_____	_____
Abl_____	_____	_____	_____	_____	_____

Masculine		Feminine		Neuter	
Latin	English Meaning(s)	Latin	English Meaning(s)	Latin	English Meaning(s)
Plural					
Nom_____	_____	_____	_____	_____	_____
Gen_____	_____	_____	_____	_____	_____
Dat_____	_____	_____	_____	_____	_____
Acc_____	_____	_____	_____	_____	_____
Abl_____	_____	_____	_____	_____	_____

8. Decline below in the singular and plural the derivative of the third person Latin personal pronoun which means **the same**.

Masculine		Feminine		Neuter	
Latin	English Meaning(s)	Latin	English Meaning(s)	Latin	English Meaning(s)
Singular					
Nom _____	_____	_____	_____	_____	_____
Gen _____	_____	_____	_____	_____	_____
Dat _____	_____	_____	_____	_____	_____
Acc _____	_____	_____	_____	_____	_____
Abl _____	_____	_____	_____	_____	_____
Plural					
Nom _____	_____	_____	_____	_____	_____
Gen _____	_____	_____	_____	_____	_____
Dat _____	_____	_____	_____	_____	_____
Acc _____	_____	_____	_____	_____	_____
Abl _____	_____	_____	_____	_____	_____

DRILL

Name _____ Section_____ Date_____

A. Translate the following in English or Latin.

a. nōbīs (abl) _____

b. idem_____

c. vestrī_____

d. vōs _____

e. mihi _____

f. eius (fem) _____

g. eō (neuter) _____

h. nostrum _____

i. eam _____

j. eī (masc) _____

k. it _____

l. of us (partitive) _____

m. I _____

n. you (sing. dir. obj.)_____

o. for you (plu.)_____

p. by her _____

q. his _____

r. for me _____

s. the same man _____

t. its _____

B. Supply the correct form of the word shown in parentheses and translate:

a. _____ (nēmō) cōpiās mittet.

_____

b. Dā _____ (ego) tempus.

_____

c. Fīlia _____ (is) bene sentit.

_____

d. Multi _____ (vōs, genitive) nunc venient.

_____

e. Mittō nēminem ad _____ (ea, feminine).

_____

C. Translate the following:

a. The same girl will send their books.

_____

b. Her dear daughter flees with a friend.

_____

c. No one of us must write.

_____

d. Give him one hour.

_____

e. You will not find it without care.

_____

PRACTICE SENTENCES

(Before translating each, read the Latin aloud twice.)

a. Hī tibi id dabunt._____

b. Ego vōbīs id dabō._____

c. Vōs eīs id dabitis._____

d. Eī idem dabō_____

e. Nōs eī ea dabimus._____

f. Ille mihi id dabit._____

g. Vōbīs librōs eius dabimus._____

h. Nōbīs librōs eōrum dabis._____

i. Pecūniam eōrum tibi dabimus._____

j. Pecūniam eius mihi dabunt._____

k. Librōs eius ad eam mittēmus._____

l. Librum eius ad tē mittam._____

m. Ille autem pecūniam eōrum ad nōs mittet. _____

_____

n. Eās cum eā mittimus._____

o. Eum cum eīs mittō._____

p. Eōs cum amīcīs eius mittēmus._____

_____

q. Tū mē cum amīcō eōrum mittēs_____

r. Vōs mēcum ad amīcum eius mittunt. _____

_____

s. Nōs tēcum in terram eōrum mittit._____

t. Tē cum eō ad mē mittent._____

12

Perfect Active System of All Verbs; Principal Parts

OBJECTIVES

1. To learn the four forms which constitute the principal parts of Latin verbs and to memorize the principal parts of the Latin verbs learned thus far.
2. To learn to conjugate the active indicative perfect, pluperfect and future perfect, i.e., the active perfect system for Latin verbs of all four conjugations.

GRAMMAR

(Memorize paradigms and vocabulary by repeating them aloud!)

1. The names of the forms which constitute the principal parts of Latin verbs listed in the sequence used in vocabularies and dictionaries are:

_____   _____   _____   _____

2. Give the principal parts for the four Latin conjugations using the pattern verbs
we have used in our text with the English meaning under each one:

1st_____ _____ _____ _____

_____ _____ _____ _____

2nd_____ _____ _____ _____

_____ _____ _____ _____

3rd_____ _____ _____ _____

_____ _____ _____ _____

3rd (iō verbs) _____ _____ _____ _____

_____ _____ _____ _____

4th_____ _____ _____ _____

_____ _____ _____ _____

3. Up to this chapter, you have learned the first two principal parts of 27 Latin
verbs in addition to five pattern verbs. Nine were from the first conjugation,
seven from the 2nd, six from the 3rd, two from 3rd (iō verbs) and three from
the 4th. Add to these the first two principal parts of the irregular verbs **sum**
and **possum**.

Give the three remaining principal parts for each verb listed.

    a. cōgitō   _____ _____ _____

    b. dō   _____ _____ _____

    c. habeō   _____ _____ _____

    d. videō   _____ _____ _____

    e. agō   _____ _____ _____

    f. scrībō   _____ _____ _____

    g. faciō   _____ _____ _____

    h. fugiō   _____ _____ _____

    i. sentiō   _____ _____ _____

    j. veniō   _____ _____ _____

4. Give the principal parts of the following:

Sum   _____ _____ _____

Possum   _____ _____ _____

5. The stem of all the active perfect tenses is that of the _____ tense; i.e. the _____ principal part.

6. The _____ tense of **esse** is used as the endings of the active indicative _____ tense; and the _____ tense of **esse** (except for the 3rd person plural) is used as the endings of the active indicative _____ tense in all conjugations.

7. Using the verbs indicated conjugate the tenses below:

Active Indicative

Perfect (Remanēre)		Pluperfect (Vīvere)		Future Perfect (Vincere)	
Latin	English	Latin	English	Latin	English
Singular					
1. ___ ___	___ ___	___ ___
2. ___ ___	___ ___	___ ___
3. ___ ___	___ ___	___ ___
Plural					
1. ___ ___	___ ___	___ ___
2. ___ ___	___ ___	___ ___
3. ___ ___	___ ___	___ ___

DRILL

Name _____ Section _____ Date _____

A. Translate the following into English or Latin.

a. Dīxeram _____ f. They fled _____

b. Mīserimus _____ g. We shall have taught _____

c. Vēnistī _____ h. She had had _____

d. Vīcerant _____ i. You saw (plur) _____

e. Vocāvērunt _____ j. I had thought _____

B. Supply the correct form of the words in parentheses and translate.

a. _____ (remanēre; 3rd person singular perfect) diū in Asiā.

_____

b. Dī ad caelum eām _____ (mittere, future perfect).

_____

c. Caesar rēgī lībertātem _____ (dare, pluperfect).

_____

d. Dē nātūrā litterās _____ (scrībere; 1st person plural, perfect). _____

e. Fīlium tuum diū _____ (vidēre; 2nd person singular,
   pluperfect). _____

C. Translate the following.

a. They conquered nature.

_____

b. You had said (plural) nothing.

_____

c. We shall have conquered old age.

_____

d. He felt much courage.

_____

e. By treachery he had preserved his nation.

_____

PRACTICE SENTENCES

(Before translating each, read the Latin <u>aloud</u> twice.)

a. Hī remānsērunt (remanent; remanēbunt; remānserant)._____

_____

b. Rēgēs Asiam vīcērunt (vincent; vincunt; vīcerant). _____

_____

c. Caesar in eandem terram vēnerat (vēnit; venit; veniet). _____

_____

d. Caesar eadem dīxit (dīcit; dīxerat; dīcet). _____

_____

e. Vōs nōbīs pācem dedistis (dabitis; dederātis). _____

_____

f. Diū vīxerat (vīxit; vīvet). _____

_____

g. Id bene fēcerās (faciēs; fēcistī; facis). _____

_____

h. Eum in eōdem locō invēnērunt (invēnerant; invenient). _____

_____

i. Deus hominibus lībertātem dederat (dedit; dat; dabit). _____

_____

j. Vōs fuistis (erātis; estis; eritis; fuerātis) virī līberī._____

_____

13

Reflexive Pronouns and Possessives; Intensive Pronoun

OBJECTIVES

1. To learn the declension and the use of the Latin reflexive pronouns.
2. To learn the use of the third person reflexive possessive adjectives *suus, -a, -um*.
3. To learn the declension and the use of the Latin intensive pronoun/adjective *ipse, -a, -um*.

GRAMMAR

(Memorize paradigms and vocabulary by repeating them aloud!)

1. Reflexive pronouns are "bent back" to reflect on the (Circle one.)

   object   verb   subject

2. Since reflexive pronouns are used only in the predicate and reflect one of the above, they have no need for which of the following cases?

   genitive   accusative   nominative

3. Give **all** the meanings of the following (include those learned in Chapter 11):

a. mihi _____

b. vōbīs _____

c. nōs _____

d. meī _____

e. sē _____

f. vōs _____

g. tē _____

h. suī _____

i. vestrī _____

j. tibi _____

k. nōbīs _____

l. nostrī _____

m. tuī _____

n. mē _____

o. sibi _____

4. Decline the Latin intensive pronoun.

Masculine		Feminine		Neuter	
Latin	English Meaning(s)	Latin	English Meaning(s)	Latin	English Meaning(s)

Singular

Nom ___ ___ | ___ ___ | ___ ___

Gen ___ ___ | ___ ___ | ___ ___

Dat ___ ___ | ___ ___ | ___ ___

Acc ___ ___ | ___ ___ | ___ ___

Abl ___ ___ | ___ ___ | ___ ___

Plural

Nom ___ ___ | ___ ___ | ___ ___

Gen ___ ___ | ___ ___ | ___ ___

Dat ___ ___ | ___ ___ | ___ ___

Acc ___ ___ | ___ ___ | ___ ___

Abl ___ ___ | ___ ___ | ___ ___

5. For the first and second persons, the Romans indicated possession by _____(my), _____(your; singular), _____ (our) and _____ (your; plural) whether the possessive adjective was used as a reflexive or not.

6. For the third person, the Romans normally indicated possession by _____ (his, her, its, their) when the possessive adjective was used in the predicate and referred to the subject. Otherwise, they regularly indicated possession by the genitives _____, _____, and _____ (literally of him, of her, of it, of them).

DRILL

Name _____**Section** _____**Date** _____

A. Supply the correct form of the words in parentheses and translate.

   a. Scrīpsit nōmen _____ (possession; masculine; refers to subj.). _____

   b. Dīxit nōmen _____ (possession; feminine; does not refer to subj.). _____

   c. Magister numquam _____ (reflexive) docuit sapientiam.
   _____

   d. Magister numquam _____ (regular personal feminine) docuit sapientiam. _____

   e. Ante bellum, cōpiae cum amīcīs _____ (his) sē iūnxērunt.
   _____

B. Translate the following:

   a. They gave themselves courage.

   _____

   b. They gave them courage.

   _____

   c. I said it to myself.

   _____

   d. They said it to me.

   _____

   e. He will preserve his (someone else's) freedom.

   _____

PRACTICE SENTENCES

(Before translating each, read the Latin <u>aloud</u> twice.)

a. Cicero came to Caesar himself

_____

b. Cicero esteemed himself and you esteem yourself.

_____

c. Caesar eum servāvit. _____

d. Caesar sē servāvit. _____

e. Rōmānī sē servāvērunt. _____

f. Rōmānī eōs servāvērunt. _____

g. Rōmānī eum servāvārunt. _____

h. Caesar amīcum suum servāvit.

_____

i. Caesar amīcum eius servāvit.

_____

j. Nōs nōn servāvērunt. _____

k. Nōs servāvimus. _____

l. Mihi nihil dedit. _____

m. Mihi nihil dedī. _____

n. Sibi nihil dedit. _____

o. Sibi nihil dedērunt. _____

p. Mē vīcī. _____

q. Mē vīcērunt. _____

14

i-stem Nouns of the Third Declension; Ablative of Means, Accompaniment and Manner

---

OBJECTIVES

1. To complete our study of the third declension of Latin nouns with the i-stem nouns.

2. To learn to recognize and understand the precise meaning of the Latin ablatives of means or instrument, of accompaniment, and of manner.

GRAMMAR

(Memorize paradigms and vocabulary by repeating them aloud!)

1. The third declension nouns we studied in Chapter 7 are known as (Circle one.)

         i-stems   Consonant stems   a-stems

2. The first group or category of third declension i-stem nouns are called parisyllabic because the nominative and genitive have the same number of syllables. The nominative ending of nouns in this group is either _____ or _____.

3. The majority of nouns in the parisyllabic group are (Circle one.)

   masculine   feminine

4. The second group or category of i-stem nouns has a stem ending in two consonants. The nominative ending of nouns in this group is either _____ or _____.

5. The third group or category of i-stem nouns contains only a few neuter nouns whose nominatives end either in _____, _____, or _____.

6. The i in the third declension i-stem nouns appears in nouns of all three genders in only one case, the (Circle one.)

   ablative singular   genitive plural   accusative plural

7. The only other consistent appearance of the i in third declension i-stem nouns is in the ablative singular and the nominative and accusative plural of which of the three groups? (Circle one.)

   First (m. + f.)   Second (m. + f.)   Third (n)

8. Give the declensions of the second declension noun **vir** and the irregular third declension **i-stem** noun **vis**.

Latin	English	Latin	English
Singular			
Nom_____ _____		_____ _____
Gen _____ _____		_____ _____
Dat _____ _____		_____ _____
Acc _____ _____		_____ _____
Abl _____ _____		_____ _____
Plural			
Nom_____ _____		_____ _____
Gen _____ _____		_____ _____
Dat _____ _____		_____ _____
Acc _____ _____		_____ _____
Abl _____ _____		_____ _____

9. The Latin ablative of means/instrument answers the question (Circle one.)

      with whom?   with what?   how?

10. The Latin ablative of manner answers the question (Circle one.)

      with whom?   with what?   how?

11. The Latin ablative of accompaniment answers the question (Circle one.)

      with whom?   with what?   how?

12. With the Latin ablative of accompaniment the English preposition **with** is rendered in Latin by (Circle one.)

      no preposition   **cum**

13. With the Latin ablative of instrument the English preposition **with** is rendered in Latin by (Circle one.)

      no preposition   **cum**

14. Give the information requested for the following:

	Translation	Type of Ablative
a. with a citizen		
b. by death		
c. with feeling		
d. with skill		
e. by sea		
f. iūre		
g. cum virīs		
h. oculīs meīs		
i. cum cūrā		
j. labōre meō		

DRILL

Name _____ Section _____ Date _____

A. Translate the following into English or Latin.

a. arte _____   k. by force_____

b. marī _____   l. of strength_____

c. partis _____   m. of citizens _____

d. animālia _____ n. with the citizens _____

e. artium_____   o. with strength_____

f. mare _____   p. seas (nominative)_____

g. urbēs _____   q. a sea (accusative) _____

h. partium _____   r. by a citizen _____

i. animālī _____   s. for the city _____

j. nūbēs_____   t. by the sea _____

B. Supply the correct form of the words in parentheses and translate.

a. Cīvēs _____ (urbs; genitive plural) bella gerunt.

_____

b. _____ (mare; accusative) tenuit.

_____

c. Cum _____ (virtūs) mortem tolerāvērunt.

_____

d. Cum _____ (ars) urbem tenuerātis.

_____

e. Rēx trāns _____ (urbs) cucurrit.

_____

C. Translate the following:

a. He managed the city with his own strength.

_____

b. The force of the seas restrained them.

_____

c. They wrote part of the opinions. _____

d. We dragged the tyrant across the city.

_____

e. Death will never possess the soul._____

PRACTICE SENTENCES

(Before translating each, read the Latin <u>aloud</u> twice.)

a. Ipsī lībertātem cīvium suōrum servāverant. _____

_____

b. Pars cīvium per urbem ad mare cucurrit. _____

_____

c. Great is the strength of the arts. _____

d. Ipse cīvitātem vī cōpiārum tenuit. _____

e. Illa animālia multōs hominēs in mare trāxērunt. _____

_____

f. Eum ad mortem trāns terram eius trāxistis. _____

_____

g. Vīs illōrum marium erat magna. _____

_____

h. Sententiās magnās pulchrāsque ex virīs antīquīs trāximus. _____

_____

i. The citizen did that with money (with care; with his own friends).

_____

j. Multa bella cum Rōmānīs gessit. _____

k. Cīvitātem magnā cum sapientiā gessērunt. _____

_____

l. Hoc magnā cum arte dīxistī. _____

m. Cum cūrā trāns urbem cucurrimus. _____

n. Magnā cum parte cīvium ad nōs vēnit. _____

_____

o. Iūra cīvium vī vincet. _____

15

Imperfect Indicative Active of the Four Conjugations; Ablative of Time

OBJECTIVES

1. To complete our study of the active voice of the indicative of all conjugations of Latin verbs by learning the conjugation of the imperfect tense.

2. To understand the use of the imperfect tense of the indicative by comparing it and its English meaning with the perfect tense and its English meaning.

3. To continue our study of the precise meaning and use of the Latin ablative with or without prepositions by learning the ablative of time.

GRAMMAR

(Memorize paradigms and vocabulary by repeating them aloud!)

1. The three elements which are used to construct the indicative imperfect tense in all Latin conjugations are the _____ stem, the _____ sign and the active _____ endings.

2. In the fourth conjugation, the _____ sign is altered by the addition of the letter _____ preceding it taken from the _____ conjugation.

3. The Latin perfect tense indicates a _____ act in the past which can, using a camera metaphor, be compared to a _____. Therefore, the English translations of **dūxī** would be _____ or _____ or _____.

4. The Latin imperfect tense indicates a _____ or _____ or _____ action in the past which can, using a camera metaphor, be compared to a _____. Therefore, English translations of **dūcēbam** would be _____ or _____ or _____.

5. In Latin expressions denoting time when or within which something occurred, the English prepositions **at, on, in** or **within** are (Circle one.)

   translated   not translated

6. To note the similarities and differences between them, conjugate the active indicative future and imperfect of the following verbs as indicated below.

Future			Imperfect		
Stem Sign	Ending	English Meaning(s)	Stem Sign	Ending	English Meaning(s)

timēre

Singular

1._____ _____ _____ | _____ _____ _____

2._____ _____ _____ | _____ _____ _____

3._____ _____ _____ | _____ _____ _____

Plural

1._____ _____ _____ | _____ _____ _____

2._____ _____ _____ | _____ _____ _____

3._____ _____ _____ | _____ _____ _____

	Future			Imperfect		
	English stem sign	English ending	Meaning(s)	stem sign	ending	Meaning(s)

mittere

Singular

1._____ _____ _____ _____ _____ _____

2._____ _____ _____ _____ _____ _____

3._____ _____ _____ _____ _____ _____

Plural

1._____ _____ _____ _____ _____ _____

2._____ _____ _____ _____ _____ _____

3._____ _____ _____ _____ _____ _____

7. Give the indicated information for the following:

	Translation	Type of Ablative
a. with the girls	_____	_____
b. with a letter	_____	_____
c. with great courage	_____	_____
d. with courage	_____	_____
e. in one hour	_____	_____
f. at the same time	_____	_____
g. within a few hours	_____	_____
h. at that time	_____	_____
i. by means of supplies	_____	_____
j. with money	_____	_____

DRILL

Name _____ Section _____ Date _____

A. Translate the following.

a. We were daring.

_____

b. She threw.

_____

c. He has taken.

_____

d. I habitually wrote.

_____

e. We used to understand.

_____

f. They came.

_____

g. I kept hearing.

_____

h. You (plur) have changed.

_____

i. They have feared.

_____

j. You (sing) were fleeing.

_____

k. They kept coming.

_____

l. They were fearing.

_____

m. We used to dare.

_____

n. You (sing) fled.

_____

o. She was throwing.

_____

p. He used to take.

_____

q. I heard.

_____

r. I wrote.

_____

s. We understood.

_____

t. You (plur) used to change.

_____

B. Supply the correct form of the words in parentheses and translate.

a. Itaque pater filiam suam _____ (exspectāre, imperfect).

_____

b. Inter cīvēs, multī sententiās suās _____ (mutāre, future). _____

_____

c. _____ (intellegere, 2nd person plural, perfect) iura?

_____

d. Italiam patribus _____ (committere, 3rd person plural, imperfect). _____

_____

e. Nautae mare numquam _____ (timēre, future).

_____

C. Translate the following.

a. They drove the tyrant out.

_____

b. You used to entrust part of the city to the troops.

_____

c. Your father understood their opinion.

_____

d. We were throwing his letter into the sea.

_____

e. By philosophy, he used to change their character.

_____

PRACTICE SENTENCES

(Before translating each, read the Latin <u>aloud</u> twice.)

a. Iste tyrannus sē semper laudābat.

_____

b. In urbem cum amīcō meō veniēbam.

_____

c. Bella magna cum virtūte gerēbātis.

_____

d. Itaque Rōmānī Graecōs vīcērunt.

_____

e. Vīdistīne patrem meum eō tempore?

_____

f. Ubi hanc pecūniam invēnistis?

_____

g. Vēnērunt, et idem nōbīs dīcēbat.

_____

h. Librōs eius numquam intellegēbam.

_____

i. Vītam nostram numquam mutāvimus.

_____

j. Rōmānī mōrēs temporum antīquōrum laudābant.

_____

16

Adjectives of the Third Declension

OBJECTIVE

To learn the declension of Latin adjectives of the third declension.

GRAMMAR

(Memorize paradigms and vocabulary by repeating them aloud!)

1. Adjectives of the third declension are declined, except in the ablative singular of the masculine and feminine, like which of the following third declension noun groups: (Circle one.)

   consonant-stem   i-stem

2. The majority of Latin third declension adjectives belong to the group having how many nominative singular endings? (Circle one.)

   one   two   three

3. The ablative singular ending for all third declension adjectives is the same as that for the neuter third declension i-stem nouns ending in **-e**, **-al**, or **-ar**. The ending is, therefore, _____.

4. Masculine and feminine third declension adjectives follow the pattern of the i-stem noun _____ and the neuter ones of the i-stem noun _____.

5. The two cases in which the characteristic i appears in all genders of the third declension adjectives are the _____ singular and the _____ plural.

6. Decline the Latin adjectives which correspond to the following:

	Powerful	
Masculine	**Feminine**	**Neuter**
Singular		
Nom_____	_____	_____
Gen _____	_____	_____
Dat _____	_____	_____
Acc _____	_____	_____
Abl _____	_____	_____
Plural		
Nom _____	_____	_____
Gen _____	_____	_____
Dat _____	_____	_____
Acc _____	_____	_____
Abl _____	_____	_____

All, Every

Masculine	Feminine	Neuter
Singular		
Nom _____	_____	_____
Gen _____	_____	_____
Dat _____	_____	_____
Acc _____	_____	_____
Abl _____	_____	_____
Plural		
Nom _____	_____	_____
Gen _____	_____	_____
Dat _____	_____	_____
Acc _____	_____	_____
Abl _____	_____	_____

Swift

Masculine	Feminine	Neuter
Singular		
Nom _____	_____	_____
Gen _____	_____	_____
Dat _____	_____	_____
Acc _____	_____	_____
Abl _____	_____	_____
Plural		
Nom _____	_____	_____
Gen _____	_____	_____
Dat _____	_____	_____
Acc _____	_____	_____
Abl _____	_____	_____

7. Can third declension adjectives be used with nouns of the first and second declension? _____.

DRILL

Name _____ **Section**_____**Date** _____

A. Translate the following:

a. omnī marī

_____

b. omnium partium

_____

c. omnia nōmina

_____

d. dulcī matrī

_____

e. omnī bonā arte

_____

f. beātae mātrī

_____

g. ommium bellōrum

_____

h. beātō hominī

_____

i. ommia maria

_____

j. dulcī puellā

_____

k. dulcī mātre

_____

l. omnia bella

_____

m. beātō homine

_____

n. omnī bonae artī

_____

o. dulcī puellae

_____

p. vī celerī

_____

q. omnī parte

_____

r. omnis bonae artis

_____

s. omnium rēgum

_____

t. beātā mātre

_____

B. Supply the correct form of the words in parentheses and translate.

a. _____ (dulcis, e) memoriae senectūtem iuvant.

_____

b. Mātrēs aetatem _____ (brevis, e) semper timēbunt.

_____

c. Quam _____ (celes, celeris, celere) sunt aetātēs!

_____ _____ _____

d. Pater amīcōs _____ (miser) filiōrum (acer) iūvit.

_____ _____ _____

e. Corpore _____ (fortis, e) saepe vincebāmus.

_____

C. Translate the following:

a. All laws are not good laws.

_____

b. We retained memories of a difficult life.

_____

c. In a short period of time the war had changed.

_____

d. Within an hour you expected every friend.

_____

e. They drew strength from the pleasant woman's courage.

_____

PRACTICE SENTENCES

(Before translating each, read the Latin <u>aloud</u> twice.)

a. Aetās longa saepe est difficilis.

_____

b. Aetās difficilis potest esse beāta.

_____

c. Quam brevis erat dulcis vīta eius!

_____

d. Memoria dulcis aetātis omnēs hominēs adiuvat

_____

e. In omnī terrā multōs virōs fortēs vidēbitis.

_____

f. Illud bellum breve erat difficile.

_____

g. Omnia perīcula paucīs hōrīs superāvimus.

_____

h. Brevī tempore omnia iūra cīvium mūtābit.

_____

i. Difficilem artem lībertātis dulcis nōn intellēxērunt.

_____

j. Hominēs officia difficilia in omnibus terrīs timent.

_____

17

The Relative Pronoun

OBJECTIVE

To learn the declension and the use of Latin relative pronouns.

GRAMMAR

(Memorize paradigms and vocabulary by repeating them aloud!)

1. A relative pronoun in English or in Latin is so called because it
   _____ or _____ to a noun or
   another pronoun called its _____ .

2. Relative clauses are parts of sentences which are termed (Circle one.)

   simple   complex

3. A relative pronoun usually begins a clause termed (Circle one.)

   principal   coordinate   subordinate

4. The term **antecedent** comes from **ante** + **cēdere** which means
   _____.

5. The case of the relative pronoun is determined by its (Circle one.)

   function in its clause   antecedent

6. The gender and number of the relative pronoun are determined by its (Circle one.)

     function in its clause   antecedent

7. Decline the Latin relative pronouns:

Masculine		**Feminine**		**Neuter**	
Latin	**English Meaning(s)**	**Latin**	**English Meaning(s)**	**Latin**	**English Meaning(s)**
Singular					
Nom_____	_____	_____	_____	_____	_____
Gen_____	_____	_____	_____	_____	_____
Dat_____	_____	_____	_____	_____	_____
Acc_____	_____	_____	_____	_____	_____
Abl_____	_____	_____	_____	_____	_____
Plural					
Nom _____	_____	_____	_____	_____	_____
Gen _____	_____	_____	_____	_____	_____
Dat _____	_____	_____	_____	_____	_____
Acc _____	_____	_____	_____	_____	_____
Abl _____	_____	_____	_____	_____	_____

DRILL

Name _____ Section _____ Date _____

A. Translate the following into English or Latin.

a. Puer cuius liber

_____

b. Oculōs quōs

_____

c. Vīrēs quibus

_____

d. Litterās quae

_____

e. Id quod

_____

f. Eam quācum

_____

g. Cīvēs quī

_____

h. Iūs quō

_____

i. Urbs per quam

_____

j. Locum quem

_____

k. The state (subj.) which (dir. obj.)

_____

l. The daughter (dir. obj.) whose

_____

m. The seas (dir. obj.) across which

_____

n. The books (subj.) in which

_____

o. The woman (subj.) to whom

_____

p. The citizen (dir. obj.) who

_____

q. The friends (dir. obj.) with whom

_____

r. The letter (subj.) which (subj.)

_____

s. The sons (subj.) whom

_____

t. The girls (dir. obj.) who

_____

B. Supply the correct form of the words in parentheses and translate.

a. Vēritās _____ (quī, quae, quod) dīxistī erat difficilis.

_____

b. Factum _____ (quī, quae, quod, ablative)
vīcimus erat magnum. _____

c. Vīderam fēminam _____ (quī, quae, quod, genitive)
fīlius fūgerat. _____

d. Sentīmus amīcitiam _____ (quī, quae, quod) sē
nōn mūtābit. _____

e. Viae trāns _____ (quī, quae, quod) currēbant erant
longae. _____

C. Translate the following:

a. The treachery which we feared is evil.

_____

b. You will lead those troops with whom you came.

_____

c. He will destroy the friendship which we have.

_____

d. They neglected the man whose deeds were great.

_____

e. The age which is beginning will be happy.

_____

PRACTICE SENTENCES

(Before translating each, read the Latin <u>aloud</u> twice.)

a. Cīvēs laudāvērunt quōs mīserātis.

_____

b. Cīvem laudāvērunt quī patriam servāverat.

_____

c. Cīvem laudāvērunt cuius fīlius patriam servāverat.

_____

d. Cīvēs laudāvērunt quōrum fīliī patriam servāverant.

_____

e. Cīvem laudāvērunt cui patriam commīserant.

_____

f. Cīvēs laudāvērunt quibus patriam commīserant.

_____

g. Tyrannus urbēs dēlēvit ex quibus cīvēs fūgerant.

_____

h. Tyrannus urbēs dēlēvit in quās cīvēs fūgerant.

_____

i. Puellīs quā laudābat librōs dedit.

_____

j. Virō cuius fīliam amās vītam suam commīsit.

_____

18

Present, Imperfect and Future Indicative Passive; Ablative of Agent

OBJECTIVES

*1. To learn the forms of the **passive voice** of the present, imperfect, and future indicative and the present infinitive of the Latin first and second conjugations.*
2. To understand the use of the passive voice.
3. To learn the function of the ablative of personal agent and its relationship with the ablative of means/instrument and the passive voice.

GRAMMAR

(Memorize paradigms and vocabulary by repeating them aloud!)

1. When a verb is in the active voice, the action is performed by the (Circle one.)

    subject   object

2. When a verb is in the passive voice, the action is performed by the (Circle one.)

    subject   object

3. When a verb is in the active voice, the action is received by the (Circle one.)

      subject   object

4. When a verb is in the passive voice, the action is received by the (Circle one.)

      subject   object

5. In the following sentences, underline the performer of the action:

    a. The player struck his opponent.
    b. The opponent was struck by the player.

6. In the following sentences, underline the receiver of the action:

    a. The player struck his opponent.
    b. The opponent was struck by the player.

7. The passive infinitive present forms of **laudō** and **moneō** are _____ and _____. The English meanings of those infinitives are _____ and _____.

8. Five of the six passive personal endings are characterized by the consonant letter _____.

9. Using the first conjugation verb **iūvāre**, conjugate the following tenses of the indicative in the passive voice:

Present		Future		Imperfect	
Latin	**English**	**Latin**	**English**	**Latin**	**English**
Singular					
1._____	_____	_____	_____	_____	_____
2._____	_____	_____	_____	_____	_____
3._____	_____	_____	_____	_____	_____

	Present		Future		Imperfect	
Latin		**English**	**Latin**	**English**	**Latin**	**English**
Plural						
1._____		_____	_____	_____	_____	_____
2._____		_____	_____	_____	_____	_____
3._____		_____	_____	_____	_____	_____

10. Using the second conjugation verb **delere**, conjugate the following tenses of the indicative in the passive voice:

	Present		Future		Imperfect	
Latin		**English**	**Latin**	**English**	**Latin**	**English**
Singular						
1._____		_____	_____	_____	_____	_____
2._____		_____	_____	_____	_____	_____
3._____		_____	_____	_____	_____	_____

	Present		Future		Imperfect	
Latin		**English**	**Latin**	**English**	**Latin**	**English**
Plural						
1._____		_____	_____	_____	_____	_____
2._____		_____	_____	_____	_____	_____
3._____		_____	_____	_____	_____	_____

11. Provide the information indicated for the following ablatives:

	Preposition (if none, so indicate)	Used for people, things, etc.
a. means/instrument	_____	_____
b. accompaniment	_____	_____
c. manner	_____	_____
d. time	_____	_____
e. personal agent	_____	_____

DRILL

Name _____ **Section** _____ **Date** _____

A. Translate the following into English or Latin.

a. Vocābiminī

_____

b. Vocābāminī

_____

c. Vocāminī

_____

d. Docēbantur

_____

e. Docentur

_____

f. Docēbuntur

_____

g. Mutābimur

_____

h. Mutābāmur

_____

i. Tenēbāris

_____

j. Tenēberis

_____

k. She used to be feared.

_____

l. She is being feared.

_____

m. She will be feared.

_____

n. I shall be expected.

_____

o. I am expected.

_____

p. I was being expected.

_____

q. We habitually were seen.

_____

r. We shall be seen.

_____

s. It is tolerated.

_____

t. It will be tolerated.

_____

B. Supply the correct passive form of the words in parentheses and translate:

a. In lūdō puellae _____ (docēre, present).

_____

b. Puerī ā magistrō nōn _____ (movēre, future).

_____

c. Omnēs urbēs ā cōpiīs _____ (dēlēre, imperfect).

_____

d. Mora cōnsiliōrum ā nōbīs _____ (expectāre, imperfect).

_____

e. Hīs generibus insidiārum _____ (servāre, 1st person plural, future).

_____

C. Translate the following:

_____

a. The school will be changed by this plan.

_____

b. We were not being helped by that type of game.

_____

c. He is not being affected even by his own father.

_____

d. You will not be feared by your citizens.

_____

e. The letter used to be held by my daughter.

_____

PRACTICE SENTENCES

(Before translating each, read the Latin *aloud* twice.)

a. Mē terrent; ab eīs terreor; vī eōrum terreor.

_____

b. Ab amīcīs movēbātur; cōnsiliīs eōrum movēbātur.

_____

c. Vīribus hominum nōn dēlēmur, sed possumus īnsidiīs dēlērī.

_____

d. Tū ipse nōn mūtāris, sed nōmen tuum mūtātur.

_____

e. Librī huius generis puerīs a magistrō dabantur sed paucī legēbantur.

_____

f. Lībertās populō ab rēge brevī tempore dabitur.

_____

g. Patria nostra ā cīvibus fortibus etiam nunc servārī potest.

_____

h. Fortūnā aliōrum monērī dēbēmus.

_____

i. Ab amīcīs potentibus adiuvābimur.

_____

j. Omnēs virōs nostrōs laudāmus, quī virtūte et vēritāte moventur, nōn amōre suī.

_____

19

Perfect Passive System of all Verbs; Interrogative Pronouns and Adjectives

OBJECTIVES

1. To learn to conjugate the passive indicative perfect, pluperfect and future perfect, i.e., the passive perfect system for Latin verbs of all four conjugations.

2. To learn to decline and to use the Latin interrogative pronouns and adjectives.

GRAMMAR

(Memorize paradigms and vocabulary by repeating them aloud!)

1. The Latin perfect passive indicative is composed of the passive
   _____ _____ and the _____ tense of **esse**.

2. The Latin pluperfect passive indicative is composed of the passive
   _____ _____and the _____ tense of **esse**.

3. The Latin passive indicative future perfect is composed of the passive
   _____ _____and the _____ tense of **esse**.

4. Conjugate the following tenses in the passive voice using the Latin verb
   amāre.

Present Latin Singular	Eng. 1	Eng. 2	Perfect Latin	Eng. 1	Eng. 2
1._____	_____	_____	_____	_____	_____
2._____	_____	_____	_____	_____	_____
3._____	_____	_____	_____	_____	_____

Present Latin Plural	Eng. 1	Eng. 2	Perfect Latin	Eng. 1	Eng. 2
1._____	_____	_____	_____	_____	_____
2._____	_____	_____	_____	_____	_____
3._____	_____	_____	_____	_____	_____

5. Conjugate the following tenses in the passive voice using the Latin verb **terrēre**.

Imperfect		**Pluperfect**	
Latin	**English**	**Latin**	**English**
Singular			
1._____	_____	_____	_____
2._____	_____	_____	_____
3._____	_____	_____	_____
Plural			
1._____	_____	_____	_____
2._____	_____	_____	_____
3._____	_____	_____	_____

6. Conjugate the following tenses in the passive voice using the latin verb **mittere**.

Future Perfect	
Latin	**English**
Plural	
1._____	_____
2._____	_____
3._____	_____

7. The declension of the Latin interrogative pronouns in the singular is almost the same as that of the _____ pronouns.

8. The singular cases of the two above types of pronouns which differ are the _____, the _____, the _____ and the _____.

9. The declension of the singular of the _____ adjectives and the _____ pronouns is exactly the same.

10. The declension of the plural of the _____ pronouns, the _____ adjectives and the _____ pronouns is exactly the same.

11. The distinctions between the following are best remembered by filling in the chart as indicated.

	Modifies noun (yes or no)	Expressed or implied antecedent (has or has not)	Introduces a direct question (yes or no)	Sentence ends with question mark (yes or no)
interr. pronoun	_____	_____	_____	_____
interr. adj.	_____	_____	_____	_____
relative pronoun	_____	_____	_____	_____

12. Fill in the following declensions.

Interr. Pronoun
Singular

M Latin	English	F Latin	English	N Latin	English
Nom _____	_____	_____	_____	_____	_____
Gen_____	_____	_____	_____	_____	_____
Dat_____	_____	_____	_____	_____	_____
Acc_____	_____	_____	_____	_____	_____
Abl_____	_____	_____	_____	_____	_____

Interr. Adjective (& Relative Pronoun)
Singular

M		F		N	
Latin	**English**	**Latin**	**English**	**Latin**	**English**
Nom_____	_____	_____	_____	_____	_____
Gen_____	_____	_____	_____	_____	_____
Dat_____	_____	_____	_____	_____	_____
Acc_____	_____	_____	_____	_____	_____
Abl_____	_____	_____	_____	_____	_____

13. Fill in the following declension.

Interr. Pronoun & Adjective (& Relative Pronoun)
Plural

M		F		N	
Latin	**English**	**Latin**	**English**	**Latin**	**English**
Nom_____	_____	_____	_____	_____	_____
Gen_____	_____	_____	_____	_____	_____
Dat_____	_____	_____	_____	_____	_____
Acc_____	_____	_____	_____	_____	_____
Abl_____	_____	_____	_____	_____	_____

DRILL

Name _____ Section_____ Date_____

A. Translate the following into English or Latin.

1. Verbs

a. dūcō (three meanings) _____

b. dūcor (two meanings) _____

c. dūxī (three meanings) _____

d. ductus, -a, -um sum (two meanings) _____

e. dūcēbam (three meanings) _____

f. dūcēbar (three meanings) _____

g. dūxeram (one meaning) _____

h. dūcam (one meaning) _____

i. dūxerō (one meaning) _____

j. ductus, -a, -um erō (one meaning) _____

k. We were taken or have been taken _____

l. We were taking _____

m. We shall take _____

n. We shall have taken _____

o. We shall have been taken _____

2. Interrogative pronouns/adjectives and relative pronouns: (give all meanings).

a. Quārum?_____

b. Quis?_____

c. Quōrum_____

d. Quid?_____

e. Quod_____

f. Quam_____

g. Quem?_____

h. Quā_____

i. Quō?_____

j. Whose (sing.)_____

k. Who? (m. nom. sing.)_____

l. What? (n. acc. sing.)_____

m. Whom? (f. sing.)_____

n. Whom (m. sing.)_____

o. Which (acc. sing.)_____

B. Supply the correct form of the words in parentheses and translate:

a. Ūnā hōrā iūdicium _____ (dare, passive pluperfect).

_____

b. Ā _____ (quis? plural) _____ (ēicere, 2nd

person plural, passive perfect)? _____

_____

c. Brevī tempore _____ (dēlēre, 1st person plural,

passive future perfect). _____

_____

d. _____ (quis? genitive plural) iūdicium _____

(parāre, passive perfect)? _____

_____

e. Ā_____ (quis? singular) _____

(līberāre, 3rd person plural, passive pluperfect)? _____

_____

C. Translate the following:

a. The old man had been neglected.

_____

b. By what new game had they been helped?

_____

c. At what time will she have been saved?

_____

d. We had been neglected by him for a long time.

_____

e. By what name were you called then?

_____

PRACTICE SENTENCES

(Before translating each, read the Latin <u>aloud</u> twice.)

a. Magister ā quō liber parātus est labōre superātur.

_____

b. Puerum quī servētus est ego ipse vīdī.

_____

c. Senem cuius fīliī servātī sunt numquam vīdī.

_____

d. Ā cīve quī missus erat pāx et lībertās laudātae sunt

_____

e. Ā cīvibus quī missī erant amīcitia laudāta est.

_____

f. Cuī liber datus est (dabātur) (datus erat)?

_____

g. Quid puerō dictum est cuī liber datus est?

_____

h. Quis servātus est? Quī puer servātus est?

_____

i. Cuius fīliī servātī sunt?

_____

j. Quis missus est?

_____

k. Quōs in urbe vīdistī?

_____

l. Quae ā tē ibi inventa sunt?

_____

m. Ā quibus hoc dictum est?

_____

n. Quōrum fīliī ab eō laudātī sunt?

_____

o. Quod perīculum vōs terret?

_____

20

Fourth Declension; Ablatives of "Place from Which" and "Separation"

OBJECTIVES

1. To learn to decline Latin nouns of the fourth declension.
2. To understand the use of the Latin ablatives used to express "place from which" and "separation."

GRAMMAR

(Memorize paradigms and vocabulary by repeating them aloud.)

1. The letter which characterizes all but two endings of the fourth declension nouns is _____.

2. The two cases whose endings do not begin with the characteristic letter are the _____ _____and the _____ _____.

3. The gender of most fourth declension Latin nouns is _____.

4. The only feminine noun of the fourth declension which occurs with any frequency is _____. It is declined like nouns of the _____ gender.

5. Neuter nouns of the fourth declension declined like **cornū** are (Circle one.)

   frequent   average   rare

6. The ablative of "place from which" emphasizes the idea of _____ and requires one of the three prepositions _____, _____, or _____.

7. The ablative of "separation" from things or people after verbs meaning **to free, to lack** or **to deprive** would be placed under which of the following columns of our ablative chart?

   No Preposition   Optional Preposition   Always Preposition

8. The ablative of separation from things with most other verbs would be placed under which of the following?

   No Preposition   Optional Preposition   Always Preposition

9. The ablative of separation from people would be placed under which of the following?

   No Preposition   Optional Preposition   Always Preposition

10. Complete the following declension (be sure to include the long vowel signs -).

Latin Singular	English	Latin	English
Nom __Metus__	_____	___Cornū____	_____
Gen_____	_____	_____	_____
Dat_____	_____	_____	_____
Acc_____	_____	_____	_____
Abl_____	_____	_____	_____
Plural			
Nom_____	_____	_____	_____
Gen_____	_____	_____	_____
Dat_____	_____	_____	_____
Acc_____	_____	_____	_____
Abl_____	_____	_____	_____

DRILL

Name _____ Section _____ Date _____

A. Translate the following into English or Latin.

a. senatuī _____

k. of the senate _____

b. versū _____

l. for the band _____

c. metuum _____

m. the enjoyment (subj.) _____

d. manūs (subject) _____

n. with verses _____

e. senatum _____

o. the horns (dir. obj.) _____

f. metibus _____

p. of the dread _____

g. versūs (dir. obj.) _____

q. with the hands _____

h. manuī _____

r. the profits (subj.) _____

i. metū _____

s. by the senate _____

j. manus _____

t. the anxiety (subj.) _____

B. Supply the correct form of the words in parentheses and translate:

a. In Graeciā _____ (metus) servitūtis superāvimus.

_____

b. Neque _____ (frūctus, plural) neque _____

(metus, plural) caruistī. _____

c. Hae _____ (manus, plural) _____ (servitūs,

singular) liberātae erant. _____

_____

d. In _____ (manus) amīci _____ (metus) carent.

_____

e. Iūdicium ā rēge contrā _____ (senātus) datum est.

_____

C. Translate the following:

a. The fear of crime has terrified the people.

_____

b. In Greece, the profits of slavery were understood.

_____

c. Important verses had been written by my son.

_____

d. Laws against crime save the citizens.

_____

e. He lacks the common friendship of the people.

_____

PRACTICE SENTENCES

(Before translating each, read the Latin <u>aloud</u> twice.)

a. Quis ad nōs eō tempore vēnit?

_____

b. Quid ab eō dictum est?

_____

c. Eōs sceleribus istīus tyrannī līberāvimus.

_____

d. Nunc omnī metū carent.

_____

e. Fīliī eōrum bonōs librōs in lūdīs nostrīs cum studiō legunt.

_____

f. Hī versūs nōbīs grātiās magnās agunt.

_____

g. Nam illī miserī nunc frūctūs pācis lībertātisque sine metū habent.

_____

h. Virī bonī cōpiā hōrum frūctuum numquam carēbunt.

_____

21

Third and Fourth Conjugations: Passive Voice of Indicative and Present Infinitive

OBJECTIVE

To learn the passive voice of the indicative and the present infinitive of the third and fourth conjugation verbs.

GRAMMAR

(Memorize paradigms and vocabulary by repeating them aloud!)

1. Give the present infinitives of the following verbs in the voice indicated:
   parō, moveō, mittō, ēiciō, inveniō.

Active

to prepare   to move   to send   to drive out to find

_____ _____ _____ _____ _____

Passive

to be prepared	to be moved	to be sent	to be driven out	to be found

_____ _____ _____ _____ _____

2. Conjugate in Latin the entire tense, voice, and mood indicated for each verb.

Singular

	I send	I am sent	I drive out	I am driven out	I find	I am found
1.	_____	_____	_____	_____	_____	_____
2.	_____	_____	_____	_____	_____	_____
3.	_____	_____	_____	_____	_____	_____

Plural

1.	_____	_____	_____	_____	_____	_____
2.	_____	_____	_____	_____	_____	_____
3.	_____	_____	_____	_____	_____	_____

3. Conjugate in Latin the entire tense, voice, and mood indicated for each verb.

Singular

I shall send	I shall be sent
1.	
2.	
3.	

Plural

1.	
2.	
3.	

I shall drive out
Singular

1._____

2._____

3._____

Plural

1._____

2._____

3._____

I shall be driven out

I shall find
Singular

1._____

2._____

3._____

Plural

1._____

2._____

3._____

I shall be found

4. Conjugate in Latin the entire tense, voice, and mood indicated for each verb.

I used to send
Singular

1._____

2._____

3._____

I used to be sent

Plural

1._____   _____

2._____   _____

3._____   _____

I used to drive out   **I used to be driven out**
Singular

1._____   _____

2._____   _____

3._____   _____

Plural

1._____   _____

2._____   _____

3._____   _____

I used to find   **I used to be found**
Singular

1._____   _____

2._____   _____

3._____   _____

Plural

1._____   _____

2._____   _____

3._____   _____

DRILL

Name _____ **Section** _____ **Date** _____

A. Translate the following into English or Latin.

a. Vincēminī

_____

k. He was commanding

_____

b. Scitur

_____

l. They were seized

_____

c. Iubēbimur

_____

m. It will be contained

_____

d. Rapiēbantur

_____

n. I am ordering

_____

e. Continēbar

_____

o. To be seized

_____

f. Sciēris

_____

p. They will be restrained

_____

g. Rapiar

_____

q. We were being carried away

_____

h. Continēbor

_____

r. It will be known

_____

i. Scīminī

_____

s. I conquer

_____

j. Sciēminī

_____

t. I am conquered

_____

B. Supply the correct form of the words in parentheses and translate.

a. Causa _____ (scīre; passive, present).

_____

b. In fīnibus _____ (continēre; passive, 1st person plural, future).

_____

c. Laudis causā versūs _____ (scrībere; passive, 3rd person plural, imperfect). _____

_____

d. Gentēs mundī ā mē _____ (iubēre; passive, present).

_____

e. Virtūte vestrā _____ (scīre; passive, 2nd person plural, future). _____

_____

C. Translate the following:

a. It will be ordered for the sake of the people.

_____

b. The territory was being seized.

_____

c. We used to write a letter often.

_____

d. The boundaries are well known.

_____

e. The people will never be restrained.

_____

PRACTICE SENTENCES

(Before translating each, read the Latin <u>aloud</u> twice.)

a. Quis mittitur (mittētur, mittēbātur, missus est)?

_____

_____

b. Ā quō hae litterae mittentur (missae sunt, mittuntur)? _____

_____

c. Quid dictum est (dīcēbātur, dīcētur, dīcitur)?

_____

_____

d. Diū neglegēris/neglegēminī (neglēctus es/neglēctī estis).

_____

e. Cīvitātis causē eum rapī iussērunt._____

_____

f. Animus eius pecūniā tangī nōn poterat._____

_____

g. Amor patriae in omnī animō sentiēbātur (sentiētur, sentītur, sēnsus est).

_____

_____

h. Amōre patriae cum aliīs cīvibus iungimur (iungēbāmur, iungēmur).

_____

i. Sapientia et vēritās in stultīs hominibus nōn invenientur (inveniuntur, inventae sunt)._____

_____

j. Sapientia etiam multā pecūniā nōn parātur (parābitur, parāta est).

_____

_____

22

Fifth Declension; Summary of Ablatives

OBJECTIVES

1. To learn to decline Latin nouns of the fifth declension.
2. To review the ablative ideas and expressions which have been studied so far.

GRAMMAR

(Memorize paradigms and vocabulary by repeating them aloud!)

1. The letter which characterizes all endings of the fifth declension nouns
   is_____.

2. The gender of fifth declension Latin nouns is_____.

3. The only exception to the above is _____
   whose gender is regularly _____.

4. Complete the declension of the following:

Singular Latin	English	Plural Latin	English
Nom ___fidēs	_____	_____	_____
Gen _____	_____	_____	_____
Dat _____	_____	_____	_____
Acc _____	_____	_____	_____
Abl _____	_____	_____	_____

5. Reconstruct the following chart of Latin ablatives, indicating what Latin prepositions, if any, are used.

Type	*Never* Prep.	Optional	*Always* Prep.
1._____	_____	_____	_____
2._____	_____	_____	_____
3._____	_____	_____	_____
4._____	_____	_____	_____
5._____	_____	_____	_____
6._____	_____	_____	_____
7._____	_____	_____	_____
8._____	_____	_____	_____

DRILL

Name _____ **Section** _____ **Date** _____

A. Translate the following into English or Latin.

a. Rērum

_____

b. Diēbus

_____

c. Speī (dative)

_____

d. Fidem

_____

e. Spēs (nom. sing.)

_____

f. Rēpūblicā

_____

g. Diē

_____

h. Spēs (acc. plur.)

_____

i. Fideī (genitive)

_____

j. Diēs (nom. plur.)

_____

k. to the republic (ind. obj.)

_____

l. with hope

_____

m. on that day

_____

n. for the faith

_____

o. in many days

_____

p. business (dir. obj.)

_____

q. uncertain hope (subj.)

_____

r. new things (dir. obj.)

_____

s. within one day

_____

t. of hopes

_____

B. Complete the following:

	Translation(s)	Type of Ablative
a. In urbe remānsit.	_____	_____
b. Ūnā hōrā veniet.	_____	_____
c. Eō tempore vēnit.	_____	_____
d. Cum eīs vēnit.	_____	_____
e. Ex urbe vēnit.	_____	_____
f. Igne carent.	_____	_____
g. Illud igne factum est.	_____	_____
h. Id ab eīs factum est.	_____	_____
i. Id cum fidē factum est.	_____	_____

C. Supply the correct form of the words in parentheses and translate.

a. _____ (fidēs) gentium fortis est.

_____

b. _____ (spēs) pācis numquam tollētur.

_____

c. Ignis animī _____ (fidēs; means) alitur.

_____

d. Multī cīvēs _____ (rēs pūblica; genitive) eripiuntur.

_____

e. Numerus _____ (diēs; genitive, plural) incertus est.

_____

PRACTICE SENTENCES

(Before translating each, read the Latin <u>aloud</u> twice.)

a. Rem pūblicam magnā cum cūrā gessit. _____

_____

b. Eō diē multās rēs cum spē parāvērunt. _____

_____

c. Paucīs diēbus Cicerō rem pūblicam ē perīculō ēripiet._____

_____

d. Omnēs rēs pūblicās metū liberāvistī._____

_____

e. Terra hominēs frūctibus bonīs alit. _____

_____

23

Participles

OBJECTIVES

1. To learn to identify and to decline the Latin active and passive present, perfect and future verbal adjectives called participles.
2. To learn the uses and translations of the Latin participles.

GRAMMAR

(Memorize paradigms and vocabulary by repeating them aloud!)

1. Latin verbs which follow the four regular conjugations and are transitive (i.e. take a direct object) have how many verbal adjectives called participles? (Circle one.)

   one   two   three   four   five   six

2. Of the Latin participles, how many are active and what are they?

   _____.

3. Of the Latin participles, how many are passive and what are they?

   _____.

4. The present stem is used to construct which Latin participles?

   Voice   **Tense**   **Ending**

5. The participial (fourth principal part) stem is used to construct which Latin participles?

Voice	Tense	Ending

6. Using the verbs indicated, fill in the following chart showing the participles of all conjugations.

Mūtāre

	Active Latin	English	Passive Latin	English
Present	_____	_____	_____	_____
Perfect	_____	_____	_____	_____
Future	_____	_____	_____	_____

Docēre

	Active Latin	English	Passive Latin	English
Present	_____	_____	_____	_____
Perfect	_____	_____	_____	_____
Future	_____	_____	_____	_____

Legere

	Active Latin	English	Passive Latin	English
Present	_____	_____	_____	_____
Perfect	_____	_____	_____	_____
Future	_____	_____	_____	_____

Rapere

	Active Latin	English	Passive Latin	English
Present	_____	_____	_____	_____
Perfect	_____	_____	_____	_____
Future	_____	_____	_____	_____

Sentīre

	Active Latin	English	Passive Latin	English
Present	_____	_____	_____	_____
Perfect	_____	_____	_____	_____
Future	_____	_____	_____	_____

7. The Latin active future participle conveys the idea that the accomplishment of an action is imminent and is translated by _____ _____ or _____.

8. The Latin passive future participle conveys the idea that an action is necessary, highly desirable, or strongly indicated and is translated by _____ or _____.

9. The active present participle is declined like the adjective_____ _____and the others like the adjective _____.

10. The tense of a Latin participle is relative to that of the_____ _____verb and is not _____. The key is to ask yourself if the action of the participle is_____ _____ with, _____ to or _____ to the action of the main verb.

11. Latin participles can often be more effectively translated by (Circle one.)

        specific English participle   **clauses or phrases fitting**
                expressions   **context**

DRILL

Name _____ **Section**_____**Date**_____

A. Translate the following into English or Latin in accordance with their tense and voice.

a. pressūrus _____

k. having been seen _____

b. premēns _____

l. about to write _____

c. cupītūrī _____

m. writing _____

d. datūrōs _____

n. fit to be seen _____

e. premendus _____

o. due to be written _____

f. cupīta _____

p. fit to be sent _____

g. dandum _____

q. seeing _____

h. cupiendī _____

r. having been written _____

i. pressus _____

s. going to send _____

j. cupientēs _____

t. about to see _____

B. Supply the correct form of the words in parentheses and translate.

a. Orātor _____ (invenīre; perfect participle) dīcere nōn potest. _____

b. Signum _____ (dare; present participle) cucurrit.

_____

c. Nōs, urbem _____ (opprimere; future active participle), cōnsilium ōrātōris audīvimus.

_____

d. Dōna _____ (cupere; perfect participle) rapuit.

_____

e. Signa _____ (vidēre, present participle), rēx intelleget.

_____

C. Translate the following:

a. The gifts, having been displayed, were sent.

_____

b. Shall we ever be happy desiring pleasant things only?

_____

c. The senate, about to change the law, feared the people.

_____

d. The city, having to be overwhelmed, was subdued by fire.

_____

e. Seeking pleasant things, we have neglected faith.

_____

PRACTICE SENTENCES

(Before translating each, read the Latin <u>aloud</u> twice.)

a. Captus nihil dīxit.

_____

b. Dōna dantibus grātiās ēgit.

_____

c. Aliquem dōna petentem nōn amō.

_____

d. Ad lūdum tuum fīlium meum docendum mīsī.

_____

e. Hīs īnsidiīs territī vītam miseram vīvēmus.

_____

f. Illī virī miserī, ā tyrannō vīsī, trāns fīnem cucurrērunt.

_____

g. Aliquem nōs timentem timēmus.

_____

h. Senex, ab amīcīs monitus, ad nōs fūgit.

_____

i. Quis hroman!īs perīculīs līberātus deīs grātiās nōn dabit?

_____

j. Fidem habentibus nihil est incertum.

_____

24

Ablative Absolute; Passive Periphrastic; Dative of Agent

OBJECTIVE

To learn the use of participles, or verbal adjectives, studied in the previous lesson in two idiomatic and very common Latin constructions:
a. The Ablative Absolute, a relatively independent phrase usually set off by commas.
b. The Passive Periphrastic (with Dative of Agent, not Ablative of Personal Agent).

GRAMMAR

(Memorize paradigms and vocabulary by repeating them aloud!)

1. A noun or a pronoun modified by a verbal adjective called a
   _____, with both those parts in the _____ case,
   constitutes an idiomatic and very common construction in Latin called
   the _____.

2. The above construction, or phrase, is so-called because it is _____
   _____ _____ the rest of the sentence. This is indicated via
   punctuation by setting the phrase off with _____.

3. The key test which the Romans applied for correctly using the above construction was that its noun or pronoun could not also appear as _____ or _____ of the verb in the main clause.

4. Two nouns or a noun and an adjective in the _____ case can be used as an ablative absolute without a word for "being" because the verb **sum** has no _____ _____.

5. Translating the ablative absolute literally often results in a clumsy, awkward English sentence. It is frequently better translated as an English subordinate clause beginning with a _____ whose choice depends on the circumstance reflected in the rest of the sentence.

6. Five subordinating conjunctions which are commonly used to translate the ablative absolute are, _____, _____, _____, _____ or _____.

7. Up to this point in our study of Latin, the idea of obligation or necessity has been expressed in Latin by the verb (ought, must) followed by an_____. If the latter were in the passive voice, the person accomplishing its action would be expressed by the ablative of _____.

8. Another construction, which the Romans often used to express the idea of obligation or necessity *in the passive voice*, was composed of the passive future participle (learned in the last lesson; also called the gerundive) with the verb_____. This construction goes by the name of _____ _____ .

9. In the above construction, because the verb **sum** is involved, the participle or gerundive functions as a _____ _____and agrees in _____, _____and _____ with the _____.

10. Since the above construction is passive, one would expect that the person accomplishing the action would be expressed by the ablative of_____; but, with this construc-tion, the Romans used instead a _____of _____with no preposition.

DRILL

Name _____ Section _____ Date _____

A. Supply the correct form of the words in parentheses and translate.

a. _____ (servus; capere, perfect passive participle),
dūcēs urbem recēpērunt. _____
_____

b. Imperium ducī _____ (quaerere, participle express-
ing necessity) est . _____

c. _____ (lībertās; recipere, perfect passive participle),
servī pācem quaesīvērunt. _____

d. Hominēs malī ducī _____ (expellere, participle ex-
pressing necessity) sunt._____

e. _____ (spēs; relinquere, perfect passive participle),
quisque fūgit. _____

B. Translate the following, using participles wherever possible.

a. When these things had been said, the leader accepted the gifts.

_____

b. That sign must be given to you.

_____

c. After the king had been banished, the senate made laws.

_____

d. These verses have to be written by a poet.

_____

e. Why did the command have to be abandoned by each person?

_____

PRACTICE SENTENCES

(Before translating each, read the Latin <u>aloud</u> twice.)

a. Bonīs virīs imperium tenentibus, rēs pūblica valēbit.

_____

b. Omnī cupiditāte pecūniae glōriaeque ex animō expulsā, ille dux sē vīcit.

_____

c. Omnēs cīvēs istum tyrannum timēbant, quī expellendus erat.

_____

d. Tyrannō superātō, cīvēs lībertātem et iūra recēpērunt.

_____

e. Multīs gentibus victīs, tōtum mundum tenēre cupīvistī.

_____

f. Servitūs omnis generis per tōtum mundum opprimenda est.

_____

g. Omnia igitur iūra cīvibus magnā cūrā cōnservanda sunt.

_____

h. Officiīs ā cīvibus relictīs, rēs pūblica in magnō perīculō erit.

_____

i. Vēritās et virtūs omnibus virīs semper quaerendae sunt.

_____

j. Vēritāte et virtūte quaesītīs, rēs pūblica cōnservāta est.

_____

25

All Infinitives Active and Passive; Indirect Statement

OBJECTIVES

To review the present active and passive infinitives and to learn in addition the perfect and future active infinitives and the perfect passive infinitive.

1. To learn how the Romans used the Latin infinitives in Indirect Statement.

GRAMMAR

(Memorize paradigms and vocabulary by repeating them aloud!)

1. The final letter which identifies the active present infinitive of a Latin verb is _____ while that which identifies the passive present is _____.

2. The active perfect infinitive of a Latin verb is composed of the _____ stem (from the _____principal part) plus the ending_____.

3. The perfect passive infinitive is composed of the _____ participle plus _____, the present infinitive of **sum**. The future active infinitive is composed of the _____ _____the participle plus _____ the present infinitive of **sum**.

4. Is the future passive infinitive a common form? (Circle one.)

yes   no

5. Using the verbs indicated, complete the following chart of infinitives for each conjugation.

Narrāre

	Active		**Passive**	
	Latin	**English**	**Latin**	**English**
Present	_____	_____	_____	_____
Perfect	_____	_____	_____	_____
Future	_____	_____	_____	_____

Terrēre

	Active		**Passive**	
	Latin	**English**	**Latin**	**English**
Present	_____	_____	_____	_____
Perfect	_____	_____	_____	_____
Future	_____	_____	_____	_____

Expellere

	Active		**Passive**	
	Latin	**English**	**Latin**	**English**
Present	_____	_____	_____	_____
Perfect	_____	_____	_____	_____
Future	_____	_____	_____	_____

Accipere

	Active		**Passive**	
	Latin	**English**	**Latin**	**English**
Present	_____	_____	_____	_____
Perfect	_____	_____	_____	_____
Future	_____	_____	_____	_____

Scīre

	Active		Passive	
	Latin	English	Latin	English
Present	_____	_____	_____	_____
Perfect	_____	_____	_____	_____
Future	_____	_____	_____	_____

6. The participles which form the passive perfect infinitive and the active future infinitive with **esse** are in form considered as _____ _____ and, therefore, agree with the _____ of the infinitive.

7. A direct statement is one that is made directly and could be placed in _____ marks.

8. An indirect statement is one that is reported indirectly and, therefore, follows verbs of four main categories or types which are those of _____, _____, _____, and _____.

9. List 6 Latin verbs which belong in the **saying** category.

   a. _____   d. _____

   b. _____   e. _____

   c. _____   f. _____

10. List 4 Latin verbs which belong in the **knowing** category.

   a. _____   c. _____

   b. _____   d. _____

   c. _____   e. _____

11. List 3 Latin verbs which belong in the **thinking** category.

   a. _____   c. _____

   b. _____

12. List 3 Latin verbs which belong in the **perceiving** category.

a. _____   c. _____

b. _____

13. Both of the following are examples of indirect statements. Sentence *a* is the one most often encountered in English. The form which is always used in Latin is (Circle the letter.)

a. I believe that he is brave.   b. I believe him to be brave.

14. In Latin indirect discourse, the subject of the infinitive is *always expressed* and is always in the _____ case. If that subject is a person represented by a pronoun and is the same person as the subject of the verb of saying, etc. in the main clause the _____ personal pronoun is used. If the subject is a different person represented by a pronoun, then the _____ _____ personal pronoun is used.

15. The tense of the infinitive in indirect statement does not depend on the _____ of the main verb but on the _____ relative to the main verb.

16. Fill in the blanks with the correct infinitive of **amō**.

a. Dīcunt eum _____ eam. (The time is "past," or prior to that of the main verb).

b. Dīcent eum _____ eam. (The time is "present," or contemporaneous, relative to that of the main verb).

c. Dīxērunt eum _____ eam. (The time is "future," or subsequent to that of the main verb).

DRILL

Name _____ **Section**_____**Date**_____

A. Translate only the verbs which could introduce an indirect statement.

a. videō_____   f. neglegō _____

b. nesciō_____   g. ostendō_____

c. parō_____   h. spērō_____

d. crēdō_____   i. iungō_____

e. terreō_____   j. putō_____

B. Translate the following into English or Latin.

a. movērī   f. to have been seen (fem. acc. plu.)

_____   _____

b. crēdidisse   g. to be about to change (masc. acc. sing.)

_____   _____

c. trāctōs esse   h. to be known

_____   _____

d. dīcī   i. to have touched

_____   _____

e. sustulisse   j. to have been sought (neuter acc. sing.)

_____   _____

C. Supply the correct form of the words in parentheses and translate.

a. Negāvit adulēscentem (esse, same time) fīlium suum.

_____

b. Crēdō mē imperium (relinquere, time after).

_____

c. Senātus nūntiāvit hostēs (venīre, time before).

_____

d. Servī dīcent sē hīc (capere, passive, time before).

_____

e. Vidēbimus dōna (dare, passive, same time).

_____

D. Translate the following.

a. I know that he will come.

_____

b. They believed that he had sent gifts.

_____

c. You will see that the school is prepared.

_____

d. The people related that they had been warned.

_____

e. We believe that the human soul is immortal.

_____

PRACTICE SENTENCES

(Before translating each, read the Latin aloud twice.)

a. Spērant vōs eum vīsūrōs esse.

_____

b. Sciō hoc ā tē factum esse.

_____

c. Nescīvī illa ab eō facta esse.

_____

d. Putābant tyrannum sibi expellendum esse.

_____

e. Crēdimus pācem omnibus ducibus quaerendam esse.

_____

f. Hostēs nostrī crēdunt omnem rem pūblicam sibi vincendam esse

_____

g. Hostēs spērant sē omnēs rēs pūblicās victūrōs esse.

_____

h. Bene sciō mē multa nescīre; nēmō enim potest omnia scīre.

_____

26

Comparison of Adjectives; Declension of Comparatives

OBJECTIVE

To learn how to form the comparative and superlative degree of adjectives in Latin and how to decline the two new forms.

GRAMMAR

(Memorize paradigms and vocabulary by repeating them aloud!)

1. The Latin adjective **clarus, -a, -um** means _____.

2. The comparative of clārus is _____ for which four translations are possible: _____,
_____, _____
_____ or _____ _____.

3. The comparative form of Latin adjectives is declined like the
_____ adjectives of the _____
declension, except that the comparatives have _____
stems and do not show the characteristic -i- of the third declension
adjectives in three places: _____, _____, and
_____.

4. The Latin adverb **magis** is used with the positive degree of certain adjectives to form the comparative degree when a _____ precedes the endings of those adjectives.

5. The Latin conjunction **quam** *after* a comparative adjective means _____ and the word or idea (or second member) following it has _____ as the corresponding word or idea (or first member) before the conjunction.

6. The superlative of **clarus** is _____, for which three translations are possible: _____, or _____ _____or _____ _____.

7. The superlative form of Latin adjectives is declined like _____ _____.

8. The Latin adverb **maxime** is used with the positive degree of certain adjectives to form the superlative degree when a _____ _____ precedes the endings of those adjectives.

9. The Latin conjunction **quam** before the superlative adjective **fortissimus** means _____.

10. Complete the following:

Positive	Comparative	Superlative
potens, -entis	_____	_____
iūcundus, -a, -um	_____	_____
perpetuus, -a, -um	_____	_____
dulcis, -e	_____	_____
sapiēns, -entis	_____	_____

DRILL

Name _____ **Section**_____**Date**_____

A. Translate the following into English or Latin.

a. iūcundiōrēs (acc.)

_____

b. gravissimum (nom.)

_____

c. breviōribus (abl.)

_____

d. turpiōra (nom.)

_____

e. difficiliōris

_____

f. incertissimīs (dat.)

_____

g. commūnius (acc.)

_____

h. magis idōneō (dat.)

_____

i. fidēlissimī (sing.)

_____

j. vēriōrum

_____

k. too short (acc. masc. sing.)

_____

l. as long as possible (gen. neut. sing.)

_____

m. happier (nom. neut. sing.)

_____

n. most suitable (acc. neut. plu.)

_____

o. very uncertain (abl. masc. sing.)

_____

p. rather bitter (dat. fem. plu.)

_____

q. more serious (acc. neut. sing.)

_____

r. sweetest (gen. fem. plu.)

_____

s. dearer (gen. fem. plu.)

_____

t. wiser (abl. masc. sing.)

_____

B. Supply the correct form of the words in parentheses and translate.

a. Vītā _____ (potēns, comparative) lūcem.

_____

b. Auctor scrīpsit versūs (acerbus, superlative).

_____

c. Memoria lūcis (clārus, superlative) remānsit.

_____

d. Crēdō eam esse (fidēlis, comparative) quam eum.

_____

e. Hostis quam (brevis, superlative) litterās mittet.

_____

C. Translate the following.

a. Send men as wise as possible.

_____

b. You will read a rather short book.

_____

c. Nothing is more certain than death.

_____

d. The danger is too serious for me.

_____

e. The most pleasant memories always remain.

_____

PRACTICE SENTENCES

(Before translating each, read the Latin <u>aloud</u> twice.)

a. Nūntiāvērunt ducem quam fortissimum vēnisse._____

_____

b. Lūce clārissimā ab omnibus vīsā, cōpiae fortissimae contrā hostēs
missae sunt._____

_____

c. Istō homine turpissimō expulsō, senātus cīvibus fidēliōribus dōna
dedit._____

_____

d. Hic auctor est clārior quam ille._____

_____

e. Quīdam dīxērunt hunc auctōrem esse clāriōrem quam illum.

_____

f. Quibusdam librīs sapientissimīs lēctīs, illa vitia turpiōra vītāvimus.

_____

_____

g. Quis est vir fēlīcissimus?_____

_____

h. Remedium vitiōrum vestrōrum vidētur difficilius._____

_____

i. Ille dux putāvit patriam esse sibi cāriōrem quam vītam._____

_____

j. Manus adulēscentium quam fidēlissimōrum senātuī quaerenda est.

_____

_____

27

Special and Irregular Comparison of Adjectives

OBJECTIVES

1. To learn to form the special superlatives of adjectives ending in -lis and -er.
2. To identify and memorize the few frequently encountered Latin adjectives whose comparison is completely irregular.
3. To learn the peculiarities of the declension of plūs.

GRAMMAR

(Memorize paradigms and vocabulary by repeating them aloud!)

1. List the six adjectives ending in **-lis** whose superlative is peculiar in form, and compare them at the top of the following page.

Positive	Comparative	Superlative
_____	_____	_____
_____	_____	_____
_____	_____	_____
_____	_____	_____
_____	_____	_____

2. Give three examples of adjectives having a masculine ending of the positive degree in **-er** which form the superlative in a special way, and compare them below.

Positive	Comparative	Superlative
_____	_____	_____
_____	_____	_____
_____	_____	_____

3. Give the Latin comparatives and superlatives from which the following English words are derived (write underneath each), and list the corresponding positive degree of the Latin word.

Positive	Comparative	Superlative
_____	pejorative _____	pessimist _____
_____	prior _____	primary _____
_____	superiority _____	summit and supremacy _____
_____	minority _____	minimize _____
_____	majority _____	maximum _____
_____	ameliorate _____	optimist _____

4. The English expression **more of (something)** is translated by the Latin neuter noun **plus** which logically governs the genitive case. It is used for the comparative of **multus** meaning **much**. It is always singular and is declined as follows:

Nom _____

Gen _____

Dat _____

Acc _____

Abl _____

5. The plural of **plūs** is used for the comparative of **multī** meaning many it is an adjective and is declined as follows:

	M + F	N
Nom	_____	_____
Gen	_____	_____
Dat	_____	_____
Acc	_____	_____
Abl	_____	_____

DRILL

Name _____ Section _____ Date _____

A. Translate the following into English or Latin.

a. bellum maius

_____

k. the best author

_____

b. liber simillimus

_____

l. the most beautiful sun

_____

c. puer minimus

_____

m. a more difficult book

_____

d. puella pulcherrima

_____

n. the very easy verses

_____

e. frūctus peior

_____

o. rather difficult work

_____

f. plūs labōris

_____

p. a freer people

_____

g. plūrēs labōrēs

_____

q. the worst reasons

_____

h. dōna prīma

_____

r. the last day

_____

i. cīvēs pessimī

_____

s. a greater friendship

_____

j. plūs laudis

_____

t. the highest heavens

_____

B. Supply the correct form of the words in parentheses and translate.

a. Lūx sōlis _____ (bonus, superlative) est.

_____

b. _____ (celer, superlative) remedium non semper

_____ (magnus, superlative) est._____

_____

c. _____ (sapiēns, comparative) virī saepe

_____ (parvus, comparative) numerum librōrum

scrībunt. _____

_ _____

d. Maiōrēs ex adulēscentibus _____ (multus, comparative, acc. sing.) exspectābant. _____

e. Senectūs _____ (difficilis, comparative) aetās
est. _____

C. Translate the following.

a. His son was older than his daughter.

_____

b. The daughter was more beautiful than her mother.

_____

c. Our ancestors called the sun a god.

_____

d. The greatest friendships are often the most difficult.

_____

e. More authors were writing about their own land.

_____

PRACTICE SENTENCES

(Before translating each, read the Latin <u>aloud</u> twice.)

a. Facillima saepe nōn sunt optiman.

_____

b. Difficilia saepe sunt maxima.

_____

c. Meliōra studia sunt difficiliōra.

_____

d. Puer minor maius dōnum accēpit.

_____

e. Plūrēs virī crēdunt hoc bellum esse peius quam prīmum bellum.

_____

f. Dux melior cum cōpiīs maiōribus veniet.

_____

g. Meliōrī ducī maius imperium et plūs pecūniae dedērunt.

_____

h. Cīvēs urbium minōrum nōn sunt meliōrēs quam eī urbium maximārum.

_____

i. Nōs nōn meliōrēs sumus quam plūrimī virī priōrum aetātum.

_____

j. Maiōrēs nostrī Apollinem (Apollō, acc.) deum sōlis appellābant.

_____

28

Subjunctive: Present Active and Passive; Jussive; Purpose

OBJECTIVES

1. To understand the idea underlying the Latin subjunctive mood.

2. To learn the conjugation of the active and passive present subjunctive in all conjugations.

3. To understand the basic principle governing the translation of Latin subjunctive situations.

4. To begin to master the use of the subjunctive by learning two situations which require it: the jussive (command idea) in independent clauses, and purpose in subordinate clauses.

GRAMMAR

(Memorize paradigms and vocabulary by repeating them aloud!)

1. The indicative mood is employed to express _____ (see chapter 1, note 1).

2. The subjunctive mood can be employed to express _____
   _____, _____, etc.

3. The English subjunctive is used (Circle one.)

   rarely   frequently

4. The Latin subjunctive is used (Circle one.)

   rarely   frequently

5. The Latin present subjunctive is formed in the first conjugation by changing the present stem vowel -a- to _____ and adding the _____ or _____ personal endings. In the three other conjugations, the vowel _____ _____ is consistently the sign of the present subjunctive active and passive.

6. Conjugate the following verbs as indicated:

Subjunctive Present

Active Amāre Singular	Vidēre	Mittere	Passive Rapere	Invenire
1._____	_____	_____	_____	_____
2._____	_____	_____	_____	_____
3._____	_____	_____	_____	_____
Plural				
1._____	_____	_____	_____	_____
2._____	_____	_____	_____	_____
3._____	_____	_____	_____	_____

7. Since there is no standard translation into English for the Latin subjunctive, one must be fashioned to reproduce its various ideas according to the _____.

8. The most prominent use of the subjunctive in independent, or main, clauses is to express the idea of a _____.

9. The above idea is rendered in Latin in the first person by using what is called the _____, in the second person by the _____, and in the third person by the _____ _____.

10. In English, the subordinate clause of purpose is usually expressed by the _____, while Latin employs the _____ mood.

11. The conjunctions which introduce Latin purpose clauses are_____ _____ for the positive and _____ for the negative.

DRILL

Name _____ Section _____ Date _____

A. Translate the indicative verb forms and label the subjunctives by person and number.

a. audīmur

_____

b. sciantur

_____

c. iubeam

_____

d. līberābiminī

_____

e. mittit

_____

f. scientur

_____

g. accipiēris (-re)

_____

h. appellātis

_____

i. līberēminī

_____

j. audiēmur

_____

k. audiāmur

_____

l. līberāminī

_____

m. acciperis (-re)

_____

n. appellētis

_____

o. sciuntur

_____

p. mittet

_____

q. iubear

_____

r. iubēbar

_____

s. accipiāris (-re)

_____

t. mittat

_____

B. Supply the correct form of the verbs in parentheses and translate.

a. Nē arma _____ (praestāre, 1st person plural, subjunctive).

_____

b. Lībertātis causā verbum suum _____ (dare, 3rd person plural, subjunctive). _____

c. Ōrātōrem _____ (audīre, 1st person plural, subjunctive) ut in pāce _____ (vīvere, 1st person plural).

_____

d. Cīvēs pessimōs expellāmus nē optimī insidiās _____ (timēre, 3rd person plural). _____

_____

e. Beneficia amīcitiae _____ (laudāre, 1st person singular, subjunctive).

_____

C. Translate the following.

a. Let him send us arms.

_____

b. They come to offer better arms. (See chapter 20, note 4)

_____

c. Let us avoid the danger of war.

_____

d. He writes those words in order that he may help the people.

_____

e. Let her read the letter in order that she may not flee.

_____

PRACTICE SENTENCES

(Before translating each, read the Latin <u>aloud</u> twice.)

a. Ille dux veniat. Eum exspectāmus. _____

_____

b. Beneficia aliīs praestat ut amētur. _____

_____

c. Haec verba fēlīcia vōbīs dīcō nē discēdātis. _____

_____

d. Patriae causā haec difficillima faciāmus. _____

_____

e. Arma parēmus nē lībertās nostra tollātur. _____

_____

f. Armīsne sōlīs lībertās nostra ē perīculō ēripiētur? _____

_____

g. Nē sapientēs librōs difficiliōrēs scrībant. _____

_____

h. Sapientiam enim ā librīs difficiliōribus nōn accipiēmus. _____

_____

i. Meliōra et maiōra faciat nē vītam miserrimam agat. _____

_____

j. Haec illī auctōrī clarissimō nārrā ut in librō eius scrībantur. _____

_____

_____

29

Imperfect Subjunctive; Present and Imperfect Subjunctive of Sum; Result

OBJECTIVES

1. To learn the conjugation of the active and passive Latin imperfect subjunctive tense in all conjugations.

2. To learn the present and imperfect subjunctive of esse and posse.

3. To understand the use of the imperfect subjunctive tense.

4. To learn the second situation in Latin subordinate clauses which governs the subjunctive: that of result.

GRAMMAR

(Memorize paradigms and vocabulary by repeating them aloud!)

1. The imperfect subjunctive, in all four regular Latin conjugations, is formed by combining, as a stem, the _____ _____ _____, or the _____prin-cipal part of a verb, with the _____ or _____ personal endings.

2. Conjugate the following verbs as indicated.

Subjunctive Imperfect

Passive Appellāre	Movēre	Vincere	Active Iacere	Sentīre
Singular				
1. _____	_____	_____	_____	_____
2. _____	_____	_____	_____	_____
3. _____	_____	_____	_____	_____
Plural				
1. _____	_____	_____	_____	_____
2. _____	_____	_____	_____	_____
3. _____	_____	_____	_____	_____

3. Conjugate the following:

Subjunctive

Present Esse	Posse	Imperfect Esse	Posse
Singular			
1. _____	_____	_____	_____
2. _____	_____	_____	_____
3. _____	_____	_____	_____
Plural			
1. _____	_____	_____	_____
2. _____	_____	_____	_____
3. _____	_____	_____	_____

4. The imperfect subjunctive has no standard English translation. The Romans used it in purpose clauses and in result clauses when the main verb was in a _____ tense.

5. In Latin sentences which include purpose or result clauses, the mood of the main verb can be _____, _____ or _____.

6. When Latin purpose or result clauses are positive, the conjunction which introduces either one is _____.

7. When Latin purpose or result clauses are negative, the conjunction which introduces a purpose clause is _____ and that which introduces a result clause is _____.

8. In Latin sentences, the presence of a result clause can often be determined by the following three indicator words found in the principal clause:

Latin Word(s)   **Meaning(s)**

a. _____   _____

b. _____   _____

c. _____   _____

DRILL

Name _____ Section _____ Date _____

A. Translate the indicative verb forms and label the subjunctives by number, person and tense.

a. vocāret

_____

b. vidērēmus

_____

c. expellēminī

_____

d. ēriperēs

_____

e. servārētis

_____

f. inveniēs

_____

g. possumus

_____

h. dīcat

_____

i. dīcit

_____

j. moventur

_____

k. posset

_____

l. vidēmus

_____

m. discēderent

_____

n. discēdant

_____

o. possīmus

_____

p. accipiās

_____

q. ēripiēs

_____

r. acciperēs

_____

s. expellerēminī

_____

t. movērentur

_____

B. Supply the correct form of the verbs in parentheses and translate.

    a. Discipulī tantōs librōs lēgērunt ut vēritātem _____
(discere, 3rd person plural). _____

_____

    b. Auctor tam bene scrīpsit ut omnēs librōs eius _____
(legere, 1st person plural). _____

    c. Adulēscēns tam dūrus erat ut amīcōs nōn _____
(habēre, 3rd person singular). _____

_____

    d. Tanta dīxit ut imperium tibi _____ (dare, 1st person plural). _____

_____

    e. Hic lūdus ita bonus est ut multa _____ (discere,
1st person singular). _____

_____

C. Translate the following.

    a. The sign was so clear that everyone saw it.

_____

    b. The laws are so harsh that there is no liberty.

_____

    c. He helped them with arms so that the city might not be conquered.

_____

    d. He wrote so well that the students learned his verses.

_____

    e. You have such a great mind that you are able to learn many things.

_____

PRACTICE SENTENCES

(Before translating each, read the Latin <u>aloud</u> twice.)

a. Bonōs librōs cum cūrā legēbāmus ut sapientiam discerēmus. _____

b. Optimī librī discipulīs legendī sunt ut vēritātem et mōrēs bonōs discant. _____
_____

c. Animī plūrimōrum hominum tam stultī sunt ut discere nōn cupiant.
_____

d. At multae mentēs ita ācrēs sunt ut bene discere possint. _____
_____

e. Ommēs cīvēs sē patriae dent nē hostēs lībertātem tollant. _____
_____
_____

f. Caesar tam ācer dux erat ut hostēs mīlitēs Rōmānōs nōn vincerent.
_____
_____

g. Tanta beneficia faciēbātis ut omnēs vōs amārent. _____
_____

h. Tam dūrus erat ut nēmō eum amāret. _____
_____

i. Multī cīvēs ex eā terrā fugiēbant nē ā tyrannō opprimerentur.
_____
_____

j. Lībertātem sīc amāvērunt ut numquam ab hostibus vincerentur.
_____
_____

30

Perfect and Pluperfect Subjunctive Active and Passive; Indirect Questions; Sequence of Tenses

OBJECTIVES

1. To learn the conjugation of the active and passive Latin perfect and pluperfect subjunctive tenses in all conjugations.

2. To review direct and indirect statements (Chapter 25), to contrast them with direct and indirect questions, and to learn the third situation in Latin subordinate clauses which requires the subjunctive: that of indirect question.

*3. To identify the indicative and subjunctive tenses which belong to the two groups known as **primary (or principal)** and **historical (or secondary)** and to learn and apply the basic rule for the use of latin tenses called **sequence of tenses**.*

GRAMMAR

(Memorize paradigms and vocabulary by repeating them aloud!)

1. Comparing the structure of the **active** perfect and pluperfect subjunctive tenses, one can see that both are constructed from the _____ stem plus the respective tense signs _____ and _____ _____ and the active personal endings.

2. Comparing the structure of the *passive* perfect and pluperfect subjunctive tenses, one can see that both are constructed from the perfect passive _____ plus the _____ or _____ subjunctive of the verb **esse**.

3. Using the verbs indicated, conjugate the following:

			Subjunctive		
Perfect Active			**Pluperfect**		
Mutāre	**Movēre**		**Trahere**	**Iacere**	**Invenīre**

Singular

1._____ _____ | _____ _____ _____

2._____ _____ | _____ _____ _____

3._____ _____ | _____ _____ _____

Plural

1._____ _____ | _____ _____ _____

2._____ _____ | _____ _____ _____

3._____ _____ | _____ _____ _____

Passive

Singular

1._____ _____ | _____ _____ _____

2._____ _____ | _____ _____ _____

3._____ _____ | _____ _____ _____

Plural

1._____ _____ | _____ _____ _____

2._____ _____ | _____ _____ _____

3._____ _____ | _____ _____ _____

4. In Latin and in English, verbs in a principal clause which precedes an indirect question are those of _____ _____, _____, _____ and _____. The word which introduces the indirect question of the subordinate clause is an _____ word. The verb of indirect questions, in Latin, is in the _____ mood.

5. The following chart is designed to illustrate the Roman way of designating tenses as **primary** or **historical** (**secondary**) and the basic rule, called **sequence of tenses,** for the use of those tenses in latin. Fill in the appropriate tenses of the subjunctive (note that you must determine whether the action indicated by the verb in the subordinate clause occurs before, after, or at the same time as the action of the verb in the principal clause):

Main Clauses

(Indicative, Imperative, or Jussive Subjunctive)

Subordinate Clauses

(Subjunctive)

**Primary Tenses
(Principal)**

Present or Future time (plus perfect for English (present perfect)

_____ (for simultaneous or subsequent time)

_____ (for prior time)

**Historical Tenses
(Secondary)**

Past time

_____ (for simultaneous or subsequent time)

_____ (for prior time)

6. Therefore, the basic rule for **sequence of tenses,** simply stated, is that a _____ tense of the subjunctive is always used with a _____ tense of the main verb and a _____ tense of the subjunctive is always used with a _____ tense of the main verb.

DRILL

Name _____ Section _____ Date _____

A. Give the voice, person, number and tense of each of the following subjunctive forms.

a. iusserim

_____

b. posueritis

_____

c amārēs

_____

d. rapiāminī

_____

e. scīvissem

_____

f. iussus essem

_____

g. rapiāmus

_____

h. pōnerētis

_____

i. amēris (-re)

_____

j. raperēmus

_____

k. amāverīs

_____

l. iussissem

_____

m. scītus sim

_____

n. posuissētis

_____

o. amārēris (-re)

_____

p. raperēminī

_____

q. scītus essem

_____

r. scīverim

_____

s. positī essētis

_____

t. iussus sim

_____

B. Supply the correct form of the verbs in parentheses and translate.

a. Rogāvit ubi ferra _____ (invenīre, passive, time prior). _____

_____

b. Mundus rogat unde malum _____ (venīre, active, time contemporaneous). _____

_____

c. Ducēs comprehendent cūr _____ (fugere, 1st person plural, active, time prior). _____

_____

d. Discesseram ut sōlem _____ (vitāre, 1st person singular, active, time contemporaneous). _____

_____

e. Pater meus exposuit cūr _____ (discēdere, 1st person singular, active, time prior). _____

_____

C. Translate the following:

a. We learned so much that we arrested the speaker.

_____

b. We will learn why the speaker has been arrested.

_____

c. The general asked whence the soldiers had come.

_____

d. He will ask when the sword was placed there.

_____

e. You know why the signal has not been given.

_____

PRACTICE SENTENCES

(Before translating each, read the Latin <u>aloud</u> twice.)

a. Nesciō ubi pecūnia posita sit.

_____

b. Scīsne ubi pecūnia ponātur?

_____

c. Scīvērunt ubi pecūnia ponerētur.

_____

d. Nescīvit ubi pecūnia posita esset.

_____

e. Ōrātor rogāvit cūr cēterī cīvēs haec cōnsilia nōn cognōvissent.

_____

f. Audīvimus cīvēs tam fidēlēs esse ut rem pūblicam cōnservārent.

_____

g. Audīvimus quid cīvēs fēcissent ut rem pūblicam cōnservārent.

_____

h. Quaerēbant quōrum in rē pūblicā pāx invenīrī posset.

_____

i. Cognōvimus pācem in Patriā eōrum nōn inventam esse.

_____

j. Illī stultī semper rogant quid sit melius quam imperium aut pecūnia.

_____

31

Cum with the Subjunctive; Fero

OBJECTIVES

1. *To learn a fourth situation in Latin subordinate clauses which usually requires the subjunctive: that involving the conjunction* **cum**.

2. *To learn the principal parts of the irregular verb* **ferre** *and those few forms which omit the connecting* **e** *or* **i** *and do not follow the 3rd conjugation paradigm of* **dūcere**.

GRAMMAR

(Memorize paradigms and vocabulary by repeating them aloud!)

1. Before this chapter, we considered the Latin word **cum** to be a
_____ whose English meaning is _____.

2. The Romans also used the word **cum** at the beginning of a subordinate clause as a conjunction which, when followed by the subjunctive, had three basic meanings: _____ when past circumstances of an event were emphasized, _____ when the cause of something was indicated, and _____ which indicated a concession and was commonly accompanied by the word _____ in the main clause.

3. The four principal parts of the Latin irregular verb **ferre** are:

_____ _____ _____ _____

4. In addition to the obviously irregular perfect and participial forms of **ferre**, the basic reason for its irregularity in other tenses is lack of the connection vowels _____ or _____. Otherwise, **ferre** belongs to the _____ conjugation and is conjugated like _____.

5. Conjugate the following tenses of **ferre**:

		Indicative		**Imperative**		**Infinitive**	
	Present Active	**Present Passive**		**Present Active**	**Active**	**Passive**	
Singular							
1. _____	_____			_____	_____		
2. _____	_____	_____					
3. _____	_____						
Plural							
1. _____	_____						
2. _____	_____	_____					
3. _____	_____	_____					

DRILL

Name _____ Section _____Date _____

A. Label the subjunctives by voice, person, number and tense and translate the remaining forms:

a. tulisse
_____

b. lātūrum esse
_____

c. ferendus
_____

d. lātum esse
_____

e. tulisset
_____

f. fertis
_____

g. ferēris (-re)
_____

h. ferris (-re)
_____

i. fer
_____

j. ferrī
_____

k. ferunt
_____

l. ferent
_____

m. ferant
_____

n. fertur
_____

o. ferte
_____

p. ferat
_____

q. fert
_____

r. ferret
_____

s. feret
_____

k. lātus eram
_____

B. Supply the correct form of the verbs in parentheses and translate.

a. Cum mediocris _____ (esse, 3rd person singular, time prior), tamen eum tolerāmus.

_____

b. Cum in exsilium _____ (mittere, passive, 3rd person plural, time contemporaneous), nullum auxilium datum est.

_____

c. Cum vīnum tibi _____ (dare, passive, time contemporaneous), tamen exsilium nōn bene fers.

_____

d. Cum apud hostēs _____ (esse, 2nd person plural, time contemporaneous), amīcī sē ad vōs nāve contulērunt.

_____

e. Cum auxilium _____ (ferre, 3rd person plural, time prior), unō annō hoc fēcimus.

_____

C. Translate the following.

a. Although the times were calm, swords were nevertheless carried.

_____

b. When the exile of the leader had been ordered, they departed.

_____

c. Because the opportunities were few, the ships were prepared.

_____

d. Since the students had been thrown out, they came to the teacher's house.

_____

e. When the ship departs, the seas will be moderate.

_____

PRACTICE SENTENCES

(Before translating each, read the Latin <u>aloud</u> twice)

a. Cum hoc dīxissēmus, illī respondērunt sē pācem aequam oblātūrōs esse._____

_____

b. Cum sē in aliam terram contulisset, tamen amīcōs novōs invēnit._____

_____

c. Cum amīcitiam nōbīs offerant, eīs auxilium offerēmus. _____

_____

d. Cum perīculum magnum esset, omnēs cōpiās et arma brevī tempore cōntulērunt. _____

_____

e. Cum exposuisset quid peteret, negāvistī tantum auxilium posse offerrī. _____

_____

f. Cum dōna iūcunda tulissent, potuī tamen īnsidiās eōrum cognōscere.

_____

_____

g. Cum cōnsilia tua nunc comprehendāmus, īnsidiās tuās nōn ferēmus.

_____

_____

h. Cum mīlitēs nostrī hostēs vīcissent, tamen eīs multa beneficia obtulerunt.

_____

_____

i. Cum cognōvisset quanta beneficia cēterī offerrent, ipse aequa beneficia obtulit. _____

_____

j. Cum consul haec verba dīxisset, senātus respondit pecūniam ad hanc rem collātam esse. _____

32

Adverbs: Formation and Comparison; Volo

OBJECTIVES

1. To learn how to construct and compare regular Latin adverbs.

2. To know the positive, comparative and superlative forms of the most often encountered irregular Latin adverbs.

3. To learn the principal parts and the irregular forms of the Latin irregular verb **velle** *and of its derivatives* **nōlle** *and* **mālle***.*

GRAMMAR

(Memorize paradigms and vocabulary by repeating them aloud!)

1. Review the comparison of adjectives in Chapters 26 and 27.

2. Regular Latin adverbs are formed, in the positive degree, by dropping the ending of the adjective and adding to the base, for declension 1 & 2, the ending _____ and, for declension 3, the ending _____. Both of these correspond to the English adverbial ending _____.

3. Regular Latin adverbs of 3rd declension adjectives whose base ends in **-nt-** do not follow the above but are simply formed by adding _____ _____ to the base.

4. The comparative of regular Latin adverbs uses the ending _____ _____ which makes the adverb identical with the comparative degree _____ ending form of the Latin adjective. In English the comparative degree of an adverb is usually formed by placing the word _____ before the positive adverb. Two other words sometimes useful in translating the Latin comparative are _____ and _____.

5. The superlative of regular Latin adverbs is formed by dropping the ending of the superlative degree of an adjective and adding to the base the ending _____. In English the superlative degree of an adverb is usually formed by placing the words _____ or _____ before the positive adverb.

6. List ten Latin adverbs having special, individual forms (along with their English meanings) which we have already learned in our vocabulary (e.g. iam, already):

Latin	English	Latin	English
a) _____ _____		f) _____ _____	
b) _____ _____		g) _____ _____	
c) _____ _____		h) _____ _____	
d) _____ _____		i) _____ _____	
e) _____ _____		j) _____ _____	

7. The comparison of irregular Latin adverbs usually follows the basic _____ _____ of the adjective.

8. The two Latin irregular verbs which are compounds of **velle** are _____ _____ and _____ which, broken down, are _____, _____ and _____, _____ _____ and _____ _____ whose meanings are _____ and _____.

DRILL

Name _____ Section _____ Date _____

A. Translate the following adverbs into English or Latin.

a. iūcundē _____   f. least _____

b. fidēlissimē _____   g. longer _____

c. breviter _____   h. badly _____

d. peius _____   i. less _____

e. fidēlius _____   j. fastest _____

B. Label the subjunctives by person, number, and tense, and translate the remaining forms.

a. volēs_____   f. velīmus _____

b. vultis_____   g. vellēmus _____

c. vīs_____   h. voluissēs _____

d. volunt_____   i. voluistī _____

e. vult _____   j. vellet _____

C. Supply the correct form of the words in parentheses and translate.

a. Custōdiae _____ (celer, adverb, superlative) sē mōvērunt.

_____

b. Lēgēs habēre _____ (sapiēns, adverb, positive) māluimus.

_____

c. Auctor aut dīvitiās aut honōrēs _____(vērus, adverb, positive) vītāre voluerat.

_____

d. Exercitū eius _____ (facilis, adverb, superlative)
victī sumus. _____

_____

_____

e. Dīvitēs plūrēs dīvitiās _____ (celer, adverb, comparative) habēre volent. _____

_____

_____

D. Translate the following.

a. They took the wealth very happily.

_____

b. Our students will learn more quickly.

_____

c. The law was rather badly read.

_____

d. Words are often harshly spoken.

_____

e. Knowledge must always be most clearly understood.

_____

PRACTICE SENTENCES

(Before translating each, read the Latin <u>aloud</u> twice.)

a. Quīdam volunt crēdere omnēs hominēs esse pārēs.

_____

b. Quīdam negant mentēs quidem omnium hominum esse pārēs.

_____

c. Hī dīvitiās celerrimē invēnērunt; illī diūtissimē erunt pauperēs.

_____

_____

d. Hic plūrimōs honōrēs quam facillimē accipere vult.

_____

e. Nōs maximē volumus scientiam quaerere.

_____

f. Cīvēs ipsī rem pūblicam melius gessērunt quam ille dux.

_____

g. Ibi terra est aequior et plūs patet.

_____

h. Tyrannus cīvēs suōs ita male opprimēbat ut semper līberī esse vellent.

_____

_____

i. Plūrima dōna līberrimē offeret ut exercitus istum tyrannum adiuvāre
   velit. _____

_____

j. Vult haec sapientius fācere nē hanc quidem occasiōnem āmittat.

_____

_____

33

Conditions

OBJECTIVE

To learn the table of conditions in order to know the moods and tenses and, therefore, the correct meaning of the various forms of the basic Latin conditional sentences.

GRAMMAR

(Memorize paradigms and vocabulary by repeating them aloud!)

1. Conditional sentences in English and in Latin include a subordinate clause called the _____ which begins in Latin with the conjunction _____ for the positive, meaning _____, and _____ for the negative, meaning _____. They also include a main clause called the _____.

2. The table below represents another possible way of cataloguing Latin conditional sentences according to the mood of the verbs. Note the basic division into two groups (above and below the bold line). The group above the line with the indicative implies that the condition will likely be fulfilled (See chapter 1, note 1). The group below the line with the subjunctive implies situations that are merely hypothetical or quite contrary to fact (i.e., less likely to become reality). Give the correct tense(s) to be used for each type of condition.

INDICATIVE MOOD (Simple Fact)

	Conditional Clause	Main Clause (Conclusion)
1. Present	_____	_____
2. Past	_____ or _____	_____ or _____
3. Future or	_____ or _____	_____

SUBJUNCTIVE MOOD (Hypothetical or Unrealizable)

1. Present (should/would) _____ _____

2. Imperfect
(contrary to fact) _____ _____

3. Pluperfect
(contrary to fact) _____ _____

4. In the **conditional** clause of the **future more vivid** above, Latin more logically has the _____ tense where English regularly has the _____ tense.

5. The future less vivid condition is nicknamed the _____ condition.

DRILL

Name _____ Section_____ Date_____

A. Supply the correct form of the verb in parentheses and translate.

a. (Subjunctive present, should/would) Sī hoc _____
(legere, 2nd person plural) _____, (discere, 2nd
person plural). _____

_____

b. _____ (Contrary to fact, pluperfect) Sī hoc
_____ (legere, 2nd person plural), _____
(discere, 2nd person plural). _____

_____

c. (Simple fact, past) Sī hoc _____ (legere, 2nd person plural), _____ (discere, 2nd person plural).

_____

d. (Contrary to fact, imperfect) Sī hoc _____(legere, 2nd
person plural), _____ (discere, 2nd person plural).

_____

e. (Future) Sī hoc _____ (legere, 2nd person plural),
_____ (discere, 2nd person plural)._____

_____

B. Translate the following.

a. If you undertake the thing, you will surrender safety.

_____

b. If you should undertake the thing, you would surrender safety.

_____

c. If you had undertaken the thing, you would have surrendered safety.

_____

d. If you undertook the thing, you surrendered safety.

_____

e. If you were undertaking the thing, you would surrender safety.

_____

PRACTICE SENTENCES

(Before translating each, read the Latin <u>aloud</u> twice.)

a. Sī ratiō dūcit, fēlīx es.

b. Sī ratiō dūcet, fēlīx eris.

c. Sī ratiō dūcat, fēlīx sīs.

d. Sī ratiō dūceret, fēlīx essēs.

e. Sī ratiō dūxisset, fēlīx fuissēs.

f. Sī pecūniam amās, sapientiā carēs.

g. Sī pecūniam amābis, sapientiā carēbis.

h. Sī pecūniam amēs, sapientiā careās.

i. Sī pecūniam amārēs, sapientiā carērēs.

j. Sī pecūniam amāvissēs, sapientiā caruissēs.

k. Sī vēritātem quaerimus, scientiam invenīmus.

l. Sī vēritātem quaerēmus, scientiam inveniēmus.

m. Sī vēritātem quaerāmus, scientiam inveniāmus.

n. Sī vēritātem quaererēmus, scientiam invenīrēmus.

o. Sī vēritātem quaesīvissēmus, scientiam invēnissēmus.

34

Deponent Verbs; Ablative with Special Deponents

OBJECTIVES

1. To learn the regular forms of Latin deponent verbs as well as the peculiarities of their participles, infinitives and imperatives.
2. To learn representative Latin semi-deponent verbs.
3. To learn representative Latin special deponent verbs which govern the ablative (of means) because they are really reflexive verbs.

GRAMMAR

(Memorize paradigms and vocabulary by repeating them aloud!)

1. Latin deponent verbs are so named from the Latin verb **dē-pōnō** which means _____. This term "deponent" indicates that the Latin _____ forms have been "laid aside" for _____ meanings. The rule for passive forms with active meanings holds except for certain forms among the _____ and the _____. The participles with active forms are the _____ and the _____. The infinitive with an active form is the _____. The participle with a passive form and a passive meaning is the _____.

2. Using the verb **loquī**, complete the following chart underlining each form in English or Latin which does not follow the basic rule for deponent verbs:

Participles

| | Active Forms in Latin | | Passive Forms in Latin | |
	Latin	English	Latin	English
Present	_____	_____	_____	_____
Perfect	_____	_____	_____	_____
Future	_____	_____	_____	_____

3. Using the verb **ūtor** complete the following chart underlining each form in English or Latin which does not follow the basic rule for deponent verbs:

Infinitives

| | Active Forms in Latin | | Passive Forms in Latin | |
	Latin	English	Latin	English
Present	_____	_____	_____	_____
Perfect	_____	_____	_____	_____
Future	_____	_____	_____	_____

4. Using the verb **cōnāri**, complete the following in the second person singular only.

Indicative

	Latin	English
Present	_____	_____
Future	_____	_____
Imperfect	_____	_____
Perfect	_____	_____
Future perfect	_____	_____
Pluperfect	_____	_____

Subjunctive

	Latin	English
Present	_____	[The English translation _____
Imperfect	_____	depends on the use of _____
Perfect	_____	the Latin subjunctive in _____
Pluperfect	_____	a given sentence] _____

5. Using the verb **ēgrēdi**, complete the following:

Present Imperative

	Latin	English
Singular	_____	_____
Plural	_____	_____

6. Semi-deponent verbs are so-called because they are _____ in the present system and _____ in the perfect system.

7. Certain deponent verbs govern the _____ case rather than the _____ case for the English direct object because they are really _____ verbs.

DRILL

Name _____ **Section**_____**Date**_____

A. Label the subjunctive forms by person, number and tense and translate the remaining forms.

a. ūsūrum esse

_____

b. patiēris

_____

c. ūsus esset

_____

d. pateris

_____

e. ūsus

_____

f. patere

_____

g. ūterētur

_____

h. patī

_____

i. ūtitur

_____

j. passī sunt

_____

k. ūtātūr

_____

l. passum esse

_____

m. ūtēur

_____

n. patientēs

_____

o. patiendum est

_____

p. patiātur

_____

q. patitur

_____

r. patiēmur

_____

s. arbitrārētur

_____

t. arbitrētur

_____

B. Supply the correct form for the verbs in parentheses and translate.

a. Ad īnsulam _____ (proficīscī, 1st person plural, future).

_____

b. Aquā _____ (ūtī, 3rd person plural, perfect).

_____

c. Puellās servāre _____ (cōnārī, 1st person singular, imperfect).

_____

d. In exsilium eum _____ (sequī, 3rd person plural, pluperfect).

_____

e. Mala eīs _____ (patī, future passive participle) sunt.

_____

C. Translate the following.

a. About to die, he dared to speak.

_____

b. We often used the island to preserve our safety.

_____

c. Having started from the city, they followed the enemy.

_____

d. They enjoy the water and fruits of that island.

_____

e. His son was born that night at a friend's house.

_____

PRACTICE SENTENCES

(Before translating each, read the Latin <u>aloud</u> twice.)

a. Arbitrāur haec mala patienda esse. _____

_____

b. Cōnābimur haec mala patī. _____

_____

c. Nisi morī vīs, patere haec mala. _____

_____

d. Maxima mala passus, homō miser mortuus est. _____

_____

e. Hīs verbīs dictīs, eum sequī ausī sumus. _____

_____

f. Haec verba locūtī, profectī sumus nē in eō locō miserō morerēmur.

_____

g. Sī quis vīnō eius generis ūtī audeat, celeriter moriātur. _____

_____

h. Eōdem diē fīlius eius nātus est et mortuus est. _____

_____

i. Omnibus opibus nostrīs ūtāmur ut patria nostra servētur. _____

_____

j. Sī melioribus librīs ūsī essent, plūra didicissent. _____

_____

35

Dative with Special Verbs; Dative with Compounds

OBJECTIVES

1. To become familiar with Latin special verbs which govern the dative case.

2. To become familiar with Latin compound verbs which govern the dative case.

GRAMMAR

[Repeat aloud a number of times the examples of special verbs which take the dative of indirect object: **credo tibi, ignosco tibi,** etc. (Chapter 35 in Text).

1. Certain special verbs in Latin govern the _____ case rather than the _____ case for the English direct object.

2. There is no satisfactory rule for knowing which Latin verbs are in the above category. Two clues for spotting them involve writing those having an English translation which includes the preposition _____and memorizing a sample _____ or _____in the _____ case after the verb.

3. One possible guide to the use of the dative with certain compound Latin verbs is that, when the simple verb (which does not itself normally take the dative) can be substituted for the compound verb, the dative case [is *or* is not] _____ likely to be used; and that, when the _____ or the _____ has by its own meaning added a special new meaning to the simple verb, the resultant compound verb may take the _____ case.

DRILL

Name _____ Section_____Date_____

A. After writing the Latin for **him** and/or **it** (from **is, ea, id**), in the correct case, after the following, translate the expression.

a. cognōscunt _____   _____

b. ignōscunt _____   _____

c. serviunt _____   _____

d. servant _____   _____

e. patiuntur _____   _____

f. invenient _____   _____

g. nocent _____   _____

h. placent _____   _____

i. iaciunt _____   _____

j. crēdunt _____   _____

k. carent _____   _____

l. hortantur _____   _____

q. sequuntur _____   _____

n. persuādent _____   _____

o. ūtuntur _____   _____

B. Supply the correct form for the words in parentheses and translate.

a. _____ (lēx, object idea) comprehendō.

_____

b. _____ (rēs pūblica, object idea) nocuērunt.

_____

c. _____ (exercitus) ūsī sumus.

_____

d. _____ (servus, plural, object idea) imperāvī.

_____

e. Praemium _____ (ego, object idea) placet.

C. Translate the following.

a. Let us obey the law.

_____

b. The guards served him well.

_____

c. They persuaded the author.

_____

d. The army spared no resources.

_____

e. A father forgives his son.

_____

PRACTICE SENTENCES

(Before translating each, read the Latin <u>aloud</u> twice.)

a. Servī aliīs hominibus serviunt. _____

_____

b. Ille servus fīliō meō servīvit et eum servāvit. _____

c. Sī quis hunc labōrem suscēpisset, multōs servāvisset. _____

_____

d. Sī Deum nōbīs ignōscere volumus, nōs dēbēmus aliīs hominibus
    ignōscere._____

_____

e. Mihi nunc nōn crēdunt, neque umquam fīliō meō crēdere volent.

_____

f. Cum bonā fidē carērēs, tibi crēdere nōn poterant. _____

_____

g. Huic ducī pāreāmus ut nōbīs parcat et urbem servet. _____

_____

h. Nisi Caesar cīvibus placēbit, vītae eius nōn parcent. _____

_____

i. Vēritātī et sapientiae semper studeāmus et pāreāmus. _____

_____

j. Optimīs rēbus semper studēte sī vērē esse fēlīcēs vultis. _____

_____

36

Jussive Noun Clauses; Fio

OBJECTIVES

1. To review Latin indirect discourse, i.e. indirect statement (Chapter 25) and indirect question (Chapter 30).

2. To review direct commands, i.e., imperative and jussive subjunctive (Chapter 28) and to learn how an indirect command is expressed in Latin by a jussive noun clause.

3. To review regular adverbial clauses of purpose (Chapter 28) since the jussive noun clause is in form identical with the purpose clause, although in use it is a noun (or substantive) clause employed as the direct object of a verb of command.

4. To learn the use of fierī as a special passive form for the verb facere.

GRAMMAR

(Memorize paradigms and vocabulary by repeating them aloud!)

1. That feature of a language which repeats a statement, question or command rather than express it directly is called _____ _____.

2. Latin verbs of saying, knowing, thinking and perceiving are often followed by a subordinate clause of _____ _____ whose verb is in the _____ mood. The subject of these clauses is not in the _____ case but in the _____ case. English clauses of this type are introduced by the conjunction _____.

3. Latin verbs of asking, saying, knowing and perceiving are often followed by a subordinate clause of _____ _____ whose verb is in the _____ mood. In Latin and in English, clauses of this type are introduced by an _____ word.

4. Direct commands are rendered in Latin in the first person by the _____ _____, in the second person by the _____ and in the third person by the _____.

5. An indirect command is usually rendered in English by an _____ clause but in Latin by a _____ _____ clause which is similar to an adverbial clause of _____ . However, since indirect commands are objects of verbs of command, they are not adverbial clauses but are _____ clauses. Both are introduced in Latin by the conjunctions _____ for the positive and _____ for the negative, and the verbs in both these clauses are in the _____ mood.

6. List six Latin verbs of command or request which can be followed by a noun clause of indirect command: _____, _____, _____, _____, _____, and _____.

DRILL

Name _____**Section**_____**Date**_____

A. Label the subjunctives by person, number and tense and translate the remaining forms.

a. faciendus

_____

b. fīāmus

_____

c. fīent

_____

d. fierem

_____

e. fīant

_____

f. fīunt

_____

g. fīēbāmus

_____

h. fīēs

_____

i. factus esse

_____

j. fierent

_____

k. fīet

_____

l. fit

_____

m. fīat

_____

n. fierētis

_____

o. fierī

_____

p. factī sīmus

_____

q. faciam

_____

r. fēcimus

_____

s. factus essēs

_____

t. facta eris

_____

B. Supply the correct form for the verbs in parentheses and translate.

a. Eīs persuāsimus nē eī _____ (nocēre, 3rd person plural).

_____

b. Eōs hortor ut _____ (accēdere, 3rd person plural).

_____

c. Ab eā quaesīveram ut mihi _____ (ignōscere, 3rd person singular).

_____

d. Imperāvit eī nē potentior _____ (fierī, 3rd person singular).

_____

e. Monēsne mē ut tibi _____ (parēre, 1st person singular)?

_____

C. Translate the following.

a. Persuade him to become the leader.

_____

b. Warm him not to have fear.

_____

c. They ordered (use imperō) him to accept the prize.

_____

d. The woman begged her daughter not to depart.

_____

e. We urged them to confess the plot without fear.

_____

PRACTICE SENTENCES

(Before translating each, read the Latin <u>aloud</u> twice.)

a. Dīxit eōs litterīs Latīnīs studēre. _____

_____

b. Dīxit cūr litterīs Latīnīs studērent. _____

_____

c. Dīxit ut litterīs Latīnīs studērent. _____

_____

d. Tē rogō cūr hoc fēcerīs. _____

_____

e. Tē rogō ut hoc faciās. _____

_____

f. Ā tē petō ut pāx fīat. _____

_____

g. Ā mē petēbant nē bellum facerem. _____

_____

h. Eum ōrāvī nē rēgī turpī pārēret. _____

_____

i. Vōs ōrāmus ut discipulī ācerrimī fīātis. _____

_____

j. Cūrāte ut hoc faciātis. _____

_____

37

Conjugation of Eo; Constructions of Place and Time

1. To learn the conjugational peculiarities of the irregular verb **ire** *in the active voice only (passive rare).*

2. To review the syntax of regular Latin place constructions with prepositions.

3. To learn the special Latin place constructions for names of cities and towns and for **domus**. *This necessarily involves learning the locative case.*

4. To review the ablative of time which was covered in Chapter 15, and to learn the use of the accusative to indicate duration of time (time how long).

GRAMMAR

(Memorize paradigms and vocabulary by repeating them aloud!)

1. Analysis of the present infinitive of the Latin irregular verb **ire** shows that its normal stem is simply the letter _____. The irregularity of the verb derives from the fact that this stem vowel becomes _____ before the initial vowel of endings beginning with _____, _____, and _____. The only conjugated forms thus affected then are two persons of the _____ indicative and all six persons of the _____ subjunctive. Other forms affected are the declined _____ and the _____ (which we shall study in Chapter 39).

2. The future of this fourth conjugation verb (is *or* is not) _____
regularly formed and has the future endings found in (Name one.)
cōgō, cūrō, fīō _____.

3. Complete the following summary of the syntax of regular Latin
expressions of place:

	Preposition(s)	Case
a. from which	_____	_____
b. where	_____	_____
c. to which	_____	_____

4. With names of cities/towns, the Romans used the special *locative case*,
whose forms coincide with other familiar declensional forms as
follows:

	Singular	Plural
a. Declension 1	_____	_____
b. Declension 2	_____	_____
c. Declension 3	_____	_____

5. Complete the following summary of the syntax of special Latin
expressions of place involving names of cities or towns.

	Preposition(s)	Case
a. where	_____	_____
b. from which	_____	_____
c. to which	_____	_____

6. Complete the following summary of the syntax of Latin expressions
of time:

	Preposition(s)	Case
a. when	_____	_____
b. within which	_____	_____
c. how long	_____	_____

DRILL

Name _____**Section**_____**Date**_____

A. Label the subjunctive by person, number and tense and translate the remaining forms.

a. iimus _____   f. ībāmus _____

b. īrēmus_____   g. itūrus esse _____

c. īssēmus_____   h. euntem_____

d. eāmus_____   i. eunt_____

e. iērunt_____   j. ībunt _____

B. Translate the following.

a. ūnum diem _____   g. domum _____

b. ūnō diē _____   h. Athēnīs _____

c. Rōmae_____   i. domī _____

d. multōs diēs_____   j. Athēnās _____

e. Rōmam _____   k. domō_____

f. in navem _____   l. in nave _____

C. Supply the correct form of the word in parentheses and translate.

a. Frāter meus _____ (Athēnae) abiit.

_____

b. _____ (Rōma) it.

_____

c. _____ (domus) abierat.

_____

d. Deinde, _____ (Athēnae) rediit.

_____

e. Dēnique, _____ (domus) pereāmus.

_____

D. Translate the following:

a. My friends left home within one hour.

_____

b. They will remain in Rome for a few days.

_____

c. Let us return to Athens in one day.

_____

d. He will go to the island on that day.

_____

e. One may say that they returned rapidly.

_____

PRACTICE SENTENCES

(Before translating each, read the Latin <u>aloud</u> twice.)

a. Paucīs hōrīs Rōmam ībimus. _____

_____

b. Nōs ad urbem īmus; illī domum eunt. _____

_____

c. Cūr domō tam celeriter abīstī? _____

_____

d. Rōmam veniunt ut cum frātre meō Athēnās eant. _____

_____

e. Ad mortem hāc ex urbe abī et perī nē ego peream. _____

_____

f. Frātre tuō Rōmae interfectō, Athēnās rediērunt. _____

_____

g. Negāvit sē velle in istā terrā multōs diēs remanēre. _____

_____

h. Dīxistī tē domum Athēnīs ūnā hōrā reditūrum esse. _____

_____

i. Eīs diēbus solitī sumus Athēnīs esse. _____

_____

j. Sī amīcīs eius Rōmae nocuissent, Rōmam brevissimō tempore redīsset.

_____

_____

38

Relative Clauses of Characteristic; Dative of Reference

OBJECTIVES

1. To review the declension of relative pronouns (already learned in Chapter 17).

2. To review regular Latin relative clauses (also learned in Chapter 17) which state a fact about the antecedent and whose verb is, therefore, in the indicative mood.

3. To review the six types, learned thus far, of Latin subordinate clauses which require the subjunctive (See Chapters 28, 29, 30, 31, 33 and 36).

4. To learn the use of the subjunctive in relative clauses of characteristic.

5. To learn the use of the dative of reference, or interest, in Latin.

GRAMMAR

(Memorize paradigms and vocabulary by repeating them aloud!)

1. The verb in regular Latin relative clauses is in the indicative mood because the clause expresses a _____ about the antecedent.

2. Complete the following by inserting the proper forms of the Latin relative pronoun.

Singular			**Plural**		
M	**F**	**N**	**M**	**F**	**N**
Nom_____	_____	_____	_____	_____	_____
Gen_____	_____	_____	_____	_____	_____
Dat_____	_____	_____	_____	_____	_____
Acc_____	_____	_____	_____	_____	_____
Abl_____	_____	_____	_____	_____	_____

3. The six types of Latin subordinate clauses already learned which require the subjunctive mood are:

   a. _____

   b. _____

   c. _____

   d. _____

   e. _____

   f. _____

4. Another type of Latin subordinate clause requiring the subjunctive mood consists of relative clauses which state a _____ of an antecedent which is _____, _____, _____, or _____.

5. Translate the following Latin main clauses which are typical of those usually preceding a relative clause of characteristic:

a. Sunt quī. _____

b. Sunt quae. _____

c. Quis est quī? _____

d. Quid est quod? _____

e. Nēmō est quī. _____

f. Nihil est quod. _____

g. Sōlus est quī. _____

6. The regular Latin dative of indirect object is considered to be _____ _____ to the verb and thus might be called the _____ _____or _____ dative. Conversely, the dative of reference, or interest, is not so essential to the _____ but is included in a sentence for an _____ _____.

7. Give three possible translations of **tibi** used in the following Latin sentence as a dative of reference or interest: Domum redīre tibi debēmus?

a. _____?

b._____?

c._____?

DRILL

Name_____**Section**_____**Date**_____

A. Supply the correct form of the verb in parentheses and translate.

    a. Sola est quae odium _____ (sentīre, present).

    _____

    b. Quis est cuius fātum certum _____ (esse, present)?

    _____

    c. Puella quae opus _____ (facere, present) ibi est.

    _____

    d. Tibi nemo erat quī odiō _____ (cōnsūmere, passive, imperfect). _____

    _____

    e. Frāter meus quī mē _____ (amāre, present) mē dēfendet. _____

    _____

B. Translate the following.

    a. There are people who do not hesitate to forgive.

    _____

    b. There are few who do not dread pain.

    _____

    c. Who is there who doubts his authority?

    _____

    d. The citizens who doubted his authority were sent away.

    _____

    e. They were the only ones who used their feet.

    _____

PRACTICE SENTENCES

(Before translating each, read the Latin <u>aloud</u> twice.)

a. At nēmō erat quī istum hominem turpem dēfenderet._____

_____

b. Quid est quod virī plūs metuant quam tyrannum?_____

_____

c. Quis est quī inter lībertātem et imperium tyrannī dubitet?_____

_____

d. Rōmae antīquae erant quī pecūniam plūs quam rem pūblicam amārent.

_____

e. Quis est quī tantum dolōrem ferre possit?_____

_____

f. Nihil sciō quod mihi facilius esse possit._____

_____

g. Ducem quaerō quem omnēs laudent._____

_____

h. Illum ducem magnum quaerō quem omnēs laudant._____

_____

i. Virīs antīquīs nihil erat quod melius esset quam virtūs et sapientia.

_____

j. Nihil metuendum est quod animō nocēre nōn possit._____

_____

39

Gerund and Gerundive

OBJECTIVES

1. To review the Latin future passive participle, or gerundive, learned in Chapter 24.

2. To learn the declension of the Latin verbal noun or gerund.

3. To learn the gerund and gerundive constructions used by the Romans.

GRAMMAR

(Memorize paradigms and vocabulary by repeating them aloud!)

1. The Latin gerundive is a _____ _____ which may be modified like a _____ and is used as an _____.

2. The Latin gerundive is declined like an _____ of the _____ declension.

3. The Latin gerund is a _____ _____ which may be modified like a _____ and is used as a _____.

4. In view of this, the gerund is declined as a _____ of the _____ declension in the oblique cases of the singular of the _____ gender. The _____ _____ _____ of the verb serves as the nominative.

5. The Latin gerund, using **vīvere**, is declined as follows:

Latin	**English**
Nom _____	_____
Gen _____	_____
Dat _____	_____
Acc _____	_____
Abl _____	_____

6. Give an English translation of each of the following sentences and underline the Latin structure which the Romans preferred:

a. Discimus legendō librōs cum curā. _____

_____

b. Discimus librīs legendīs cum curā. _____

_____

DRILL

Name _____ Section _____ Date _____

A. Identify the following verb forms as gerunds or gerundives.

a. operibus faciendīs. _____

b. dēlendī causā _____

c. iniūriam oppugnandam _____

d. audiendō vōcem _____

e. cognōscendī lēgem _____

f. aedificiōrum dēlendōrum _____

g. lēgis cognōscendae _____

h. oppugnandum iniūriam _____

i. vōce audiendā _____

j. spēs vivendi _____

B. Supply the correct form of the verbs in parentheses and translate.

a. Aedificiī _____ (vidēre, gerundive) cupidī erāmus.

_____

b. Ars _____ (scrībere, gerund) laudābātur.

_____

c. Hoc dictum est contrā versūs _____
   (scrībere, gerundive).

_____

d. Ad pācem _____ (petere, gerundive) venient.

_____

e. Timor _____ (īre, gerund) domum vērus erat.

_____

C. Translate the following.

a. We came for the sake of hearing your voice. (gerundive)

_____

b. Reading is necessary. ("gerund" - See chapter 39, note 3)

_____

c. They saw him after reading the letter. (gerundive)

_____

d. By reading we become wise. (gerund)

_____

e. He spoke in favor of (prō) freeing the city. (gerundive)

_____

PRACTICE SENTENCES

(Before translating each, read the Latin <u>aloud</u> twice.)

a. Experiendō discimus. _____

_____

b. Sē discendō dedit. _____

_____

c. Discendī causā ad lūdum tuum vēnērunt. _____

_____

d. Metus moriendī eum terrēbat. _____

_____

e. Spēs vīvendī post mortem multōs hortātur. _____

_____

f. Cōgitandō eōs superāvit. _____

_____

g. Sē dedit litterīs Latīnīs discendīs. _____

_____

h. Librum scrīpsit dē lībertāte dēfendendā. _____

_____

i. Sapientiōrēs fīmus vītā experiendā. _____

_____

j. Multum tempus cōnsūmpsit in hīs operibus faciendīs. _____

_____

40

Numerals; Genitive of the Whole

OBJECTIVES

1. To learn the peculiarities of Latin cardinal and ordinal numerals.
2. To learn the use of the Latin genitive of the whole, or partitive genitive.

GRAMMAR

(Memorize paradigms and vocabulary by repeating them aloud!)

1. When a Latin partitive word (i.e. one indicating *a part* of a whole) is accompanied by a word indicating the whole, the word indicating *the whole* is put in the _____ case. The construction is called the _____ of the _____ or_____ _____.

2. The genitive of the whole is often encountered in Latin with the neuter nominative and accusative of certain _____ _____ or _____.

3. The genitive of the whole may itself be the neuter singular of a _____ declension _____.

4. Latin cardinal numerals from _____
   through _____ and the word meaning
   _____one thousand are _____ad-
   jectives.

5. The Latin cardinal numerals _____,
   _____, and _____, as well as
   the hundreds from _____ through
   _____ are _____ adjectives.

6. The Latin word for the plural "thousands" is _____.
   It is an _____ _____ of the
   _____ declension. It is followed by the
   _____ of the _____ when there is need
   to express the idea of the whole.

7. All cardinal numerals other than **mīlia** and the word
   _____ word are followed by the prepositions
   _____or _____ and the
   _____ case when it is necessary to express the idea
   of the whole.

8. Latin ordinal numbers are declinable adjectives of the _____
   _____ and _____ declensions.

9. Decline the Latin cardinal numerals two and three. (Plural only for obvious reason).

| Two | | | | Three | | |
M	F	N	M	F	N
Nom_____	_____	_____	_____	_____	_____
Gen_____	_____	_____	_____	_____	_____
Dat_____	_____	_____	_____	_____	_____
Acc_____	_____	_____	_____	_____	_____
Abl_____	_____	_____	_____	_____	_____

10. The genitive of ūnus, -a, -um is _____ _____ _____ and the dative is _____ _____ _____.

DRILL

Name _____ **Section**_____**Date**_____

A. Translate the following.

a. decem cīvēs   _____

b. trēs ex sex cīvibus   _____

c. centum cīvēs   _____

d. centum ex cīvibus   _____

e. tria mīlia cīvium   _____

f. quīdam ex cīvibus   _____

g. quid speī?   _____

h. minus metūs   _____

i. nihil aquae   _____

j. satis auxiliī   _____

B. Supply the correct form of the nouns in parentheses and translate.

a. Mīlle _____ (vōx, plural) audientur.

_____

b. Multa mīlia _____ (vōx, plural) audientur.

_____

c. _____ (duo) capita non habēmus.

_____

d. _____ (tertius) hominem reperient.

_____

e. Post _____ (septem) annōs, rediērunt.

_____

C. Translate the following.

a. Four of the slaves served three masters.

_____

b. One of the masters knows.

_____

c. It is necessary to send a thousand men.

_____

d. The author wrote fourteen verses.

_____

e. I read the fourteenth verse.

_____

PRACTICE SENTENCES

(Before translating each, read the Latin <u>aloud</u> twice.)

a. Salvē, mī amīce. Quid agis; Quid novī est:

---

b. Salvē et tū. Bene. Nihil novī.

---

c. Vīsne audīre aliquid bonī? Satis dīvitiārum dēnique accēpī!

---

d. At quid bonī est in dīvitiīs sōlīs? Satisne etiam sapientiae habēs?

---

e. Plūrimī autem virī dīvitēs multum metūs sentiunt.

---

f. Pauperēs saepe sunt fēlīciōrēs et minus metūs habent.

---

g. Novem ex ducibus nōs hortātī sunt ut plūs auxiliī praestārēmus.

---

h. Numquam satis ōtiī habēbit; at aliquid ōtiī melius est quam nihil.

---

i. Nostrīs temporibus omnēs plūs metūs et minus speī habēmus.

---

j. Magna fidēs et virtūs omnibus virīs reperiendae sunt.

Answer Key

CHAPTER 1

GRAMMAR

1. pronouns
2. endings
3.

-ō -m	I	-mus	we
-s	you	-tis	you
-t	he/she/it	-nt	they

4. laudāre
5. monēre

6. infinitives
   a. 2 to see to understand
   b. 1 to give
   c. 2 to be strong or well
   d. 1 to think to plan
   e. 2 to owe ought to must

   f. 1 to love to like
   g. 1 to save to keep
   h. 1 to call to summon
   i. 1 to conserve to preserve
   j. 1 to err to be mistaken to wander

7.

-re	infinitive	lauda-	mone

8.

dō	I give	I am giving	I do give
dās	you give	you are giving	you do give
dat	he/she/it gives	he/she/it is giving	he/she/it does give
dāmus	we give	we are giving	we do give
dātis	you give	you are giving	you do give
dant	they give	they are giving	they do give

9.

dēbeō	I owe/have to	I am owinghaving to	I do owehave to
dēbēs	you owe/have to	you are owing/having to	you do owe/have to
dēbet	he/she/it owes/has to	he/she/it is owing/having to	he/she/it does owe/have to
dēbēmus	we owe/have to	we are owinghaving to	we do owe/have to
dēbētis	you owe/have to	you are owing/having to	we do owe/have to
dēbent	they owe/have to	they are owing/having to	they do owe/have to

10. paradigms

DRILL

A.

a. 2 sing.	pres.	imper.	act.	call
b. 2 plur.	pres.	imper.	act.	farewell
c. 2 plur.	pres.	imper.	act.	see

d. 2 sing.	pres.	imper.	act.	give
e. 2 sing.	pres.	imper.	act.	think
f. 2 plur.	pres.	imper.	act.	think
g. 2 sing.	pres.	imper.	act.	farewell
h. 2 sing.	pres.	imper.	act.	see
i. 2 plur.	pres.	imper.	act.	give
j. 2 plur.	pres.	imper.	act.	call

B.
a. 3 sing.	pres.	indic.	act.	he/she/it calls
b. 1 plur.	pres.	indic.	act.	we think
c. 3 plur.	pres.	indic.	act.	they love
d. 2 sing.	pres.	indic.	act.	you owemust
e. 3 sing.	pres.	indic.	act.	heshe sees
f. 3 plur.	pres.	indic.	act.	they see
g. 1 plur.	pres.	indic.	act.	we owemust
h. 2 sing.	pres.	indic.	act.	you are well
i. 2 plur.	pres.	indic.	act.	you give
j. 2 sing.	pres.	indic.	act.	you love

C.
a. errātis	You often make a mistake.
b. Vidēmus	We see nothing.
c. Amat	Heshe loves me.
d. vidētis	What do you see?
e. errant	Call me if they make a mistake.
f. Dātis	You are giving nothing.
g. servamus	What are we preserving.?
h. dat	He/she/it often gives nothing.
i. amant	They love/like me
j. vidēs	Warn me if you see nothing.

PRACTICE SENTENCES

a. They warn me if I make a mistake.
b. He warns me if they make a mistake.
c. Warn me if he/she makes a mistake.
d. You have to/must warn me.
e. You have to/must save me.
f. They must not praise me.
g. What does he give? He often gives nothing.
h. They often call me and warn me.
i. I see nothing. What do you see.
j. Praise me if I do not make a mistake.
k. If you are well, we are well.
l. If he is strong, I am strong.
m. If he likes me, he must praise me.
n. Preserve me.
o. I do not have to make a mistake.
p. What must we praise.
q. He sees; he thinks; he advises.

CHAPTER 2

GRAMMAR

1. non-existent
2. a. accusative
   b. genitive
   c. nominative
   d. ablative
   e. vocative

   f. ablative
   g. dative or ablative
   h. ablative
   i. ablative
   j. ablative (locative)

3.

accusative	plural	direct object	none
	singular	direct address	none
accusative	singular	direct object	none
	plural	direct address	none
	singular	indirect object	tofor
	singular	subject	none
ablative	singular	indirect object	bywithfrometc.
	plural	indirect object	bywithfrometc.
	singular	complement of noun	of
	plural	subject	none
	plural	indirect object	tofor
genitive	plural	complement of noun	of

4.

poēta, ae, m.	poet
nauta, ae, m.	sailor
agricola, ae, m.	farmer

5.

	nominative	money
pecūniae	genitive	of money
pecūniae	dative	to/for money
pecūniam	accusative	money
pecūniā	ablative	bywithfrom money
pecūnia	vocative	[money]
	nominative	moniesfunds
pecūniārum	genitive	of moniesfunds
pecūniīs	dative	tofor monies
pecūniās	accusative	monies
pecūniīs	ablative	bywithfrom monies
pecūniae	vocative	[monies]

6.

a.	form, shape	direct object	none
b.	fame, rumor	subject	none
c.	fortunes	direct object	none
d.	angers	subject	none
e.	to/for philosophy	indirect object	to/for
f.	to/for/by/with/from the girls	indirect object	to/for/by/with/from
g.	money	subject	none
h.	of life	complement of noun	of
i.	of penalties	complement of noun	of
j.	to/for/by/with/from the countries	indirect object	to/for/by/with/from

DRILL

a. Puella		The girl is thinking.
b. pecūniam		Give the money.
c. irā		He/she counsels (advises) without anger.
d. fōrmas		We see the forms (shapes).
e. Nautae	poenas	The sailors are giving penalties (assessing punishments).
f. vitam	puellas	You love life and girls.
g. multā pecūniā		He/she is without much money.
h. patriam		You are not saving the country.
i. Fortūna		Opportunity is calling (Fortune calls).
j. philosophiam antiquam		I praise the old philosophy.
k. vītae		They are preserving your philosophy of life.
l. portārum		The shape of the doors is old (outdated).

PRACTICE SENTENCES

a. Farewell, my country.
b. The girl s luck is great.
c. The girl is praising the fortune (luck) of your country.
d. Girl, save your country.
e. Many girls love money.
f. You give the girl nothing (nothing to the girl).
g. He/she sees the girl s money.
h. You do not see the girls money.
i. We must warn (advise) the girls.
j. They must praise the girl.
k. Life brings luck to many girls.
l. You preserve my life with (by) your money.
m. Fame is nothing without fortune.
n. You do not love life without money.
o. A country is not strong without fame and fortune.
p. You must not praise the girls anger.
q. We love life without trials (penalties/difficulties).
r. Without philosophy, we are nothing.
s. What is life without philosophy?

CHAPTER 3

GRAMMAR

1. (crucial)
2. (secondary)

3. 1	5	4	3	2

4. (suspense)
5. (masculine)

6.		singular	indirect object	bywithfrometc.
	accusative	singular	direct object	none
		singular	indirect object	tofor
		plural	direct address	none
	genitive	plural	complement of noun	of
	nominative	singular	subject	none
	accusative	plural	direct object	none

1	5	4	3	2
	genitive	singular	complement of noun	of
	vocative	singular	direct address	none
		plural	indirect object	by with from etc.
		plural	subject	none
		plural	indirect object	to/for

7. a. genitive   complement of noun   of my sons
    b.   indirect object   by with from my sons
    c.   complement of noun   of the Roman people
    d.   indirect object   to/for the Roman people
    e.   indirect object   by with from Roman men
    f.   subject   great (big) men
    g. genitive   complement of noun   of Roman men
    h. genitive   complement of noun   of a few friends
    i.   indirect object   tofor my friends
    j.   indirect object   by with from my friend
    k.   direct address   Roman friends!
    l.   indirect object   by with from many boys
    m. accusative   direct object   a great (big) man
    n. nominative   subject   my boy
    o. accusative   direct object   many fields
    p. genitive   complement of noun   of a great (large) number
    q.   subject   my numbers
    r. genitive   complement of noun   of my boys
    s. nominative   subject   the Roman people
    t. vocative   direct address   great friend!

DRILL

A. a. sapientiam   We always have wisdom.
    b. puerōrum   A number of boys make mistakes.
    c. fīlīs meīs   He/she gives (conveys) wisdom to my sons.
    d. numerum magnum   virōrum magnōrum   A few boys see a large number of great men.
    e. virōs   magnae sapientiae   Call (Summon) men of great wisdom.

B. a. Sapientia virōrum magna est.
    b. Populus fīliīs Romanōrum multam pecūniam dat.
    c. Fīlus meus puellam videt.
    d. Amicōs puerī laudāmus.
    e. Multī virī magnam sapientiam philosophiae non amant.

PRACTICE SENTENCES

a. Farewell (goodbye), my friend.
b. The Roman people praise your son s wisdom.
c. O great man, save the Roman people.
d. The number of Roman peopl;e is large.
e. Many boys love girls.
f. You give my son nothing.
g. I see men in the field.
h. You see my son s friend.
i. He/she does not see your sons friend.
j. We must warn (advise) my sons.
k. They must praise your son.

l. Life brings fame to few men.
m. You number (have) me among (in the number of) your friends.
n. Great men often have few friends.
o. My friend is always thinking.
p. The son of a great man is not always a great man.
q. We do not always see (understand/perceive) the wisdomn of great men.
r. You must praise the philosophy, the wisdom of great men.

CHAPTER 4

GRAMMAR

1. (Declension 2 masculine)
2. (Neuter)
3. (Nominative & accusative)
4.

genitive	plural	complement of noun	of
genitive	singular	complement of noun	of
	singular	direct object	none
	plural	indirect object	by/with/from etc.
	singular	indirect object	by/with/from etc.
	singular	subject	none
	plural	direct object	none
	plural	indirect object	to/for
	singular	indirect object	to/for
	plural	subject	none

5. gender
6.

	nominative	a/the true service (real duty)
officiī verī	genitive	of a/the true service
officiō verō	dative	to/for true service
officium vērum	accusative	a/the true service
offīciō verō	ablative	by/with/from a/the true service
officia vēra	nominative	the real duties
officiōrum vērōrum	genitive	of the real duties
officiīs verīs	dative	to/for the real duties
officia vēra	accusative	the real duties
officiīs verīs	ablative	by/with/from the real duties

7.

of the gifts	complement of noun
of a/the plan	complement of noun
to/for/by/with/from a/the service (duty)	indirect object
to/for/by/with/from the dangers	indirect object
the wars	subject/direct object

8. (identical)
9. (predicate)
10. gender
11. a. we are
  b. they are (there are)
  c. I am
  d. You are
  e. he/she/it is (there is)
  f. You are

DRILL

A. a. perīculum vērum g. otiō magnō
  b. a/the great peace (leisure)
  c. the bad (evil) wars
  d. the pretty (beautiful) gifts
  e. (dē) consiliō stultō
  f. of a/the real danger

  h. bellum malum
  i. donīs bellīs
  j. the foolish (stupid) plans
  k. officiōrum parvōrum
  l. to/for/by/with/from a/the small service

B. a. Perīcula   vēra   The dangers are real.
  b. bellī   parvum   The danger of war is small.
  c. bellī   The boy and the girl are pretty.
  d. bona   Service (duty) and leisure (peace) are good.
  e. cūras   moras   I see concerns (visualize problems) and delays.

C. a. Bellum est malum.
  b. Otium est bonum.
  c. Magister officium amat.
  d. Oculī tuī sunt bellī.
  e. Perīculum morārum est vērum.

PRACTICE SENTENCES

a. Many wars do not preserve (insure) peace.
b. Even leisure often involves perils.
c. A foolish man praises the dangers of war.
d. We do not often preserve (insure) peace by war.
e. The Roman people do not always have a reliable peace.
f. They often preserve (save) the country and the peace by small wars.
g. Without delay, we must direct our attention to duty.
h. The danger is great.
i. We are in great danger.
j. Life is not without many dangers.
k. My friend is a man of high office.
l. The duties of the teacher are many and great.
m. You are a man of little leisure.
n. You are men of great caution.
o. Without eyes, life is nothing.

CHAPTER 5

GRAMMAR

1. -re	-re	laudā-	monē-
2. stem	future tense sign	ending	
3. -ō	-mus	-ō	-mus
-s	-tis	-s	-tis
-t	-nt	-t	-nt
4. -b-	-bi-	-b-	-bi-
-bi-	-bi-	-bi-	-bi-
-bi-	-bu-	-bi-	-bu-

5. vocābō	I shall call	habēbō	I shall have
vocābis	you will call	habēbis	you will have
vocābit	he/she/it will call	habēbit	he/she/it will have
vocābimus	we shall call	habēbimus	we shall have
vocābitis	you will call	habēbitis	you will have
vocābunt	they will call	habēbunt	they will have

6. nominative feminine   nominative neuter

7. līberī	līberae	līberī	nostrī	nostrae	nostrī
līberō	līberae	līberō	nostrō	nostrae	nostro
līberum	līberam	līberum	nostrum	nostram	nostrum
līberō	lībera	līberō	nostrō	nostrā	nostrō
līberī	līberae	lībera	nostrī	nostrae	nostra
līberōrum	līberārum	līberōrum	nostrōrum	nostrārum	nostrōrum
līberīs	līberīs	līberīs	nostrīs	nostrīs	nostrīs
līberos	līberas	lībera	nostros	nostras	nostra
līberīs	līberīs	līberīs	nostrīs	nostrīs	nostrīs

DRILL

A. a. we shall like
  b. he/she/it will be strong/well
  c. they will see
  d. we shall overcome
  e. I shall think/consider

  f. habēbō
  g. habēbitis
  h. errābit
  i. dabimus
  j. remānebunt

B. a. superābunt — Courage will conquer.
  b. Superābimus — We shall overcome the dangers.
  c. valēbit — Wisdom will be strong enoughprevail.
  d. Dabitis — You will bring glory to a friend.
  e. remānēbit — Then our fault/guilt will remain.
  f. errābunt — The girl and the boy will be wrongmistakenerr.
  g. Videbō — I shall see the teachers.
  h. remanēbunt — Delays and caresconcerns will remain.
  i. Cōgitābis — You will think aboutconsider philosophy.
  j. superabō — Because of the war, therefore, I shall conquer you.

PRACTICE SENTENCES

a. Our teacher praises me and will praise you.
b. Free men will overcome our dangerssurmount our perils.
c. Our sons love beautiful girls.
d. We have and we shall always have many guilts.
e. Our beautiful country is free.
f. You are free men you will have a beautiful country.
g. Free teachers will give care/pay attention to duty.
h. If you conquer/overcome your anger, you will conquer/overcome yourself.
i. On account ofbecause of your courage, many people/men are free.
j. Doesn't your mind/soul have enough wisdom=

CHAPTER 6

GRAMMAR

1. posse
2. complement/complete
3. uses that of **Dēbēre** or **Posse**
4. sum -I am

es - you are	erō - I shall be	eram - I was
est - he/she/it is	eris - you will be	eras - you were
sumus - we are	erit - he/she/it will be	erat - he/she/it was
estis - you are	erimus - we shall be	erāmus - we were
sunt - they are	eritis - you will be	erātis - you were
	erunt - they will be	erant - they were

5. possum - I can/am able to

potes - you can	poterō - I shall be able to	poteram - I could/was able to
potest - he/she/it can	poteris - you will be able to	poterās - You could
possumus - we can	poterit - he/she/it will be able to	poterat - he/she/it could
potestis - you can	poterimus - we shall be able to	poterāmus - we could
possunt - they can	poteritis - you will be able to	poterātis - you could
	poterunt - they will be able to	poterant - they could

DRILL

A.
a. he/she/it/there was
b. he/she/it will be able to
c. we were able to
d. I shall be
e. they will be able to
f. poterimus
g. possum
h. poterās/poterātis
i. erit
j. erāmus

B.
a. erant — The books of the Greeks were true.
b. erit — Your book will be true.
c. sunt — Our books are true.
d. poterāmus — We were not able/could not.
e. poterimus — We shall not be able to allow/tolerate evil books.
f. possumus — We cannot tolerate your faults.
g. poterās — Where were you able to conquer the tyrants? There.
h. potes — Where can you overcome the tyrants' treachery? There.
i. poteris — Where will you be able to overcome our treachery? There.
j. erant — The treachery of the Greeks was continuous.

PRACTICE SENTENCES

a. Your country was free.
b. Your friend will be a tyrant.
c. Where there is a tyrant, men cannot be free.
d. Tyrants will always have many vices.
e. We must conquer our tyrant.
f. You will be able to understand the dangers of a tyrant.
g. You will not tolerate the tyrants' treachery.
h. You must warn free men about tyrants.
i. Good and true books were able to/could save a country/nation.
j. Tyrants will not be able to overcome the wisdom of good books.

CHAPTER 7

GRAMMAR

1. masculine   feminine
2. (cannot)

3. 1. genitive   plural   masculine/feminine/neuter
   2. dative/ablative   plural   masculine/feminine/neuter
   3. nominative/accusative plural   neuter
   4. nominative/accusative plural   masculine/feminine
   5. genitive   singular   masculine/feminine/neuter
   6. accusative   singular   masculine/feminine
   7. ablative   singular   masculine/feminine/neuter
   8. dative   singular   masculine/feminine/neuter

4. a. magnum   f. magna
   b. magna   g. magnus
   c. magnus   h. magnum
   d. magna   i. magna
   e. magnus   j. magnus

DRILL

A. a. many chores/tasks
   b. of lasting peace
   c. of small states
   d. by/with/from a small state
   e. bad times

   f. magnās virtūtēs
   g. magna virtūte
   h. tempora nostra
   i. temporibus nostris
   j. amore meō

B. a. pacem
   b. Mōrēs   hominum
   c. virtūtem
   d. labore   virtūs
   e. temporis
   f. litteris   amorem
   g. virgines
   h. pacem   civitātibus
   i. laboris mōrēs homīnibus
   j. virtūte

We shall dare to preserve the peace.
The character of man is bad.
Because of (our) courage, we shall dare to remain there.
In work/labor, there is value/worth/merit.
You will not have enough time.
Without a letter, we cannot preserve love.
Greek maidens were beautiful.
We do not have peace in the states.
The habit of work will always give men character.
Won't you be able to conquer without courage?

PRACTICE SENTENCES

a. Money is nothing without good character.
b. The character of a good man will be good.
c. They will give a letter to the man.
d. We see much love of money in many men.
e. Our state will bring/give peace to many men.
f. Without a good peace, the states of our times will not be strong.
g. In many states and territories, peace could not be strong.
h. The pretty maiden loves friends of good character.
i. Men of great courage will dare to conquer the tyrants.
j. Love of country is strong in our state.

CHAPTER 8

GRAMMAR

1. i   o   u
2. a   e
3. duc   dic   fac
 ducite   dicite   facite
 fer   mitte   pone
 ferte   mittite   ponite

4. a. present plural 1   g. present singular 1
 b. future singular 2   h. future plural 3
 c. present plural 3   i. present singular 3
 d. future singular 3   j. future plural 2
 e. present plural 2   k. present singular 2
 f. future plural 1   l. future singular 1

DRILL

A. a. they will send   m. ponunt
 b. they send/are sending/do send n. ponēmus
 c. send   o. ponē
 d. we send/are sending/do send p. ponit
 e. you will send   q. ponent
 f. he does/is doing   r. ponam
 g. I shall do   s. ponis
 h. we shall do   t. ponetis
 i. you do/are doing   u. ponite
 j. he will write   v. ponimus
 k. write   w. ponitis
 l. you write/are writing   x. ponet

B. a. agit   Reason guides/leads/drives men.
 b. Scribe   Write nothing about the troops/resources.
 c. mittam   After the war, I shall send a letter.
 d. Mittit   He sends/is sending a lot of/a supply of books.
 e. agetis   You will thank your friend.

C. a. Aude bonam rationem tolerāre.
 b. Ad gloriam copias ducet/aget.
 c. Civitas tyrannō gratias aget.
 d. Amicus tuus litteras mittit.
 e. Propter laborem tuum/vestrum, copiam pecūniae habebis/habebitis.

PRACTICE SENTENCES

a. They are bringing/leading the man to/toward me.
b. Bring the man to me and I shall thank the man.
c. While the tyrant leads the troops, we can doaccomplish nothing.
d. We shall write books about peace.
e. The boys are not thanking the teacher.
f. Few people will thank our state.
g. The tyrant will lead great/a large body of troops out of/from our state.
h. A great abundance of money does not lead men to wisdom.
i. Don't we often lead/direct men to reason/judgment.
j. Judgment/reason can lead/direct men to a good life.

CHAPTER 9

GRAMMAR

1. point out — demonstratives
2. nominative — genitive — dative
3. 1 & 2 — magnus, a, um

	case	number	gender	meaning
4. a.	nominative/accusative	singular	neuter	that
b.	nominative	plural	masculine	those
	dative	singular	masculine/feminine/neuter	to/for that
c.	dative/ablative	plural	masculine/feminine/neuter	to/for/by/with/from those
d.	genitive	singular	masculine/feminine/neuter	of that
e.	ablative	singular	masculine/neuter	by/with/from that
f.	genitive	plural	feminine	of those
g.	nominative	plural	masculine	those
	dative	singular	masculine/feminine/neuter	to/for that
h.	nominative	singular	masculine	that
i.	nominative/accusative	singular/plural	feminine/neuter	that/those
j.	accusative	singular	masculine	that
k.	nominative/accusative	singular/plural	feminine/neuter	this/these
l.	genitive	singular	masculine/feminine/neuter	of this
m.	nominative/accusative	singular	neuter	this
n.	dative	singular	masculine/feminine/neuter	tofor this
o.	accusative	singular	masculine	this
p.	genitive	plural	masculine/neuter	of these
q.	nominative	singular	masculine	that
r.	accusative	plural	masculine	these
s.	accusative	singular	feminine	that
t.	nominative	plural	feminine	those
5. a.	genitive	singular	masculine/feminine/neuter	of any
b.	genitive	singular	masculine/feminine/neuter	of no, none
c.	accusative	singular	feminine	no, none
d.	ablative	singular	masculine/neuter	by/with/from any
e.	ablative	singular	masculine/neuter	by/with/from all
f.	genitive	singular	masculine/feminine/neuter	of all
g.	nominative	plural	masculine	all
	dative	singular	masculine/feminine/neuter	tofor all
h.	ablative	singular	masculine/neuter	by/with/from the only
i.	nominative	plural	masculine	only
	dative	singular	masculine/feminine/neuter	tofor the only
j.	nominative/accusative	singular	masculine/neuter	only
k.	genitive	singular	masculine/feminine/neuter	of one
l.	nominative/accusative	singular	masculine/neuter	one
m.	nominative	plural	masculine	ones
	dative	singular	masculine/feminine/neuter	tofor one
n.	genitive	singular	masculine/feminine/neuter	of the other/another
o.	nominative	plural	masculine	others
	dative	singular	masculine/feminine/neuter	to/for another
p.	ablative	singular	feminine	by/with/from another
q.	nominative/accusative	singular	neuter	another
r.	nominative	plural	masculine	the others
	dative	singular	masculine/feminine/neuter	to/for the other

s. genitive   plural   masculine/neuter   of the other(s)
t. nominative/accusative singular   masculine/neuter   the other

DRILL

A. a. this girl
    b. that girl
    c. to/for this time
    d. of this time
    e. to/for that boy
    f. to/for no book
    g. to/for this state only/nation alone
    h. of the whole/entire country
    i. of no judgment/reason
    j. of this state only/nation alone

    k. nūllam ratiōnem
    l. tōti pātriae
    m. uni cīvitati
    n. nūllos lībros
    o. aliō lībrō
    p. illī puerō solī
    q. illa/ista tempora
    r. istud/illud tempus
    s. illīus puellae solīus
    t. unī puellae

B. a. Tōtus
    b. nūlla
    c. sōla
    d. istius
    e. huius

    The entire/whole/All of the passage was true.
    You have no faults.
    We shall see only the good places.
    The fame/notoriety of that place remains.
    Many passages of this book are in error.

C. a. Nūllus locus hārum litterārum vērus est.
    b. Alius amīcus filiō meō grātiās aget.
    c. Dūc/Ducite copiās tuās/vestrās in loca illa/ista.
    d. Sine ūllā ratiōne, vocābunt.
    e. Oculī tuī illa loca vidēbunt.

PRACTICE SENTENCES

a. These men will lead/govern (lead/are leading/do lead) the whole/entire country.
b. In that book, that woman will write (I will write) those (things) about this man.
c. One man leads (will lead) those troops into this land/country.
d. We are writing (shall write) this book about another war.
e. The whole country thanks (will thank) this man alone.
f. This man alone was able to/could warn me about the crimes of this tyrant.
g. You have no troops in the other country/land.
h. Those men alone see no dangers in this plan.
i. You dare to praise not only the character but also the treachery of that man.
j. Because of the treachery, in fact, of one man, this state is not strong.

CHAPTER 10

GRAMMAR

1. a. 3   to live   k. 1   to err
   b. 4   to find   l. 3   to write
   c. 2   to be strong/worth   m. 2   to teach
   d. 1   to call   n. 4   to hear
   e. 2   to see/understand   o. 3   to lead
   f. 3i   to flee/avoid   p. 3   to do/lead
   g. 4   to come   q. 2   to dare
   h. 3i   to make/do   r. 1   to tolerate
   i. 1   to save/preserve   s. 2   to remain/stay
   j. 3i   to take/get   t. 2   to have

2. I live I flee I come
vīvis you live fugis you flee venīs you come
vīvit he/she/it lives fugit he/she/it flees venit he/she/it comes
vīvimus we live fugimus we flee venīmus we come
vīvitis you live fugitis you flee venītis you come
vīvunt they live fugiunt they flee veniunt they come
3. agam faciam inveniam
you will act agēs you will make faciēs you will find inveniēs
he/she/it will act aget he/she/it will make faciet he/she/it will find inveniet
we shall act agēmus we shall make faciēmus we shall find inveniēmus
you will act agētis you will make faciētis you will find inveniētis
they will act agent they will make facient they will find invenient

4. scrībe vīve audī
scrībite vīvite audīte

DRILL

A. a. write!
  b. we flee
  c. you will find
  d. they will live
  e. you make
  f. we come
  g. you do
  h. they take
  i. hear!
  j. lead!
B. a. fugit
  b. Vivēmus
  c. inveniet
  d. inveniet
  e. fugiunt
C. a. Amor tē inveniet.
  b. Hōra fugit.
  c. Saepe tē vidēre veniunt.
  d. Fīlia nostra in nātūrā pācem invenit.
  e. Bonam viam faciēs/faciētis.

k .dūcam
l. capiet
m. audiēmus
n. agētis
o. faciō
p. venit
q. vīvimus
r. fugitis
s. invenī!
t. scrībite!
Time flies.
We shall always live in peace.
The wisdom of old age will find peace.
Nature will find a way.
With our daughter, they are fleeing toward the road.

PRACTICE SENTENCES

a. Flee with your daughter.
b. Time flies the hours are fleeing old age is coming.
c. They are coming into your country.
d. You will find your daughter in that state.
e. The tyrant finds/discovers a road into this state.
f. We are coming toward you with large forces.
g. That man is always waging/making war.
h. Many men are doing those things but are not doing these things.
i. I shall make/compose a large amount of books.
j. You will find in the books of ancient men much philosophy and wisdom.

CHAPTER 11

GRAMMAR

1. (one)
2. (three)
3. (a)
4. (partitive genitives)
5. (objective genitives)

6.
ego	I	tū	you
meī	of me	tuī	of you
mihi	to/for me	tibi	to/for you
me	me	tē	you
me	by/with/from me	tē	by/with/from you
nōs	we	vōs	you
nostrum/nostrī	of us	vestrumvestrī	of you
nōbīs	to/for us	vōbīs	tofor you
nōs	us	vōs	you
nōbīs	by/with/from us	vōbīs	by/with/from you

7.
is	he	ea	she	id	it
eius	of him/his	eius	of her/her	eius	of it/its
eī	to/for him	eī	to/for her	eī	to/for it
eum	him	eam	her	id	it
eō	by/with/from him	ea	by/with/from her	eo	by/with/from it
eī/iī	they	eae	they	ea	they
eōrum	of them/their	earum	of them/their	eorum	of them/their
eīs	to/for them	eīs	to/for them	eīs	to/for them
eōs	them	eas	them	ea	them
eīs	by/with/from them	eīs	by/with/from them	eīs	by/with/from them

8.
īdem	the same	eadem	the same	idem	the same
eiusdem	of the same	eiusdem	of the same	eiusdem	of the same
eīdem	to/for the same	eīdem	to/for the same	eīdem	to/for the same
eundem	the same	eandem	the same	idem	the same
eōdem	by/with/from the same	eadem	by/with/from the same	eōdem	by/with/from the same
eīdem	the same	eaedem	the same	eadem	the same
eōrundem	of the same	eārundem	of the same	eōrundem	of the same
eīsdem	to/for the same	eīsdem	to/for the same	eīsdem	to/for the same
eosdem	the same	eāsdem	the same	eōsdem	the same
eīsdem	by/with/from the same	eīsdem	by/with/from the same	eīsdem	by/with/from the same

DRILL

A.
a. by/with/from us
b. the same (thing)
c. of you (objective)
d. you
e. to/for me
f. of her/her
g. by/with/from it
h. of us (partitive)
k. id
l. nostrum
m. ego
n. tē
o. vōbīs
p. eā
q. eius (suus, a, um)
r. mihi

i. her	s. ĭdemeundem
j. to/for him	t. eius (suus, a, um)

B. a. Nēmō	No one will send troops.
b. mihi	Give me time.
c. eius	His/Her daughter feels well.
d. vestrum	Many of you will come now.
e. eam	I am sending no one to her.

C. a. Eadem puella librōs eōrum mittet.
   b. Cāra fĭlia eius (sua) cum amĭcō fugit.
   c. Nēmō nostrum scrĭbere dēbet.
   d. Dā eĭ unam hōram.
   e. Sine curā id non inveniēs/inveniētis.

PRACTICE SENTENCES

a. These men will give it to you.
b. I shall give it to you.
c. You will give it to them.
d. I shall give the same thing to her/him/it.
e. We shall give them/these things to him/her/it.
f. That man will give it to me.
g. We shall give you his/her books.
h. You will give us their books.
i. We shall give you their money.
j. They will give me his/her money.
k. We shall send his/her books to you.
l. I shall send his/her book to you.
m. That man, however, will send us their money.
n. We are sending them/these women/those women with her.
o. I am sending him with them.
p. We shall send them with his/her friends.
q. You will send me with their friend.
r. They are sending you with me to his/her friend.
s. He/She is sending us with you into/to their country.
t. They will send you with him/it to me.

CHAPTER 12

GRAMMAR

1. present indicative (1st pers. sing.)	infinitive present (1st pers. sing.)	perfect indicative	perfect passive participle
2. laudō	laudāre	laudāvĭ	laudātum
I praise	to praise	I praised	praised
I am praising		I have praised	having been praised
I do praise		I did praise	
moneō	monēre	monuĭ	monitum
I warn	to warn	I warned	warned
I am warning		I have warned	having been warned
I do warn		I did warn	
dūcō	dūcere	dūxĭ	ductum

I lead	to lead	I led	led
I am leading		I have led	having been led
I do lead		I did lead	
capiō	capere	cēpī	captum
I take	to take	I took	taken
I am taking		I have taken	having been taken
I do take		I did take	
audiō	audīre	audīvī	audītum
I hear	to hear	I heard	heard
I am hearing		I have heard	having been heard
I do hear		I did hear	

3.
cōgitāre	cōgitāvī	cōgitātum
dare	dedī	dātum
habēre	habuī	habitum
vidēre	vīdī	vīsum
agere	ēgī	āctum
scrībere	scrīpsī	scrīptum
facere	fēcī	factum
fugere	fūgī	fugitum
sentīre	sēnsī	sēnsum
venīre	vēnī	ventum

4.
esse	fuī	futūrus
posse	potuī	

5. perfect   third

6. imperfect   pluperfect   future   future perfect

7.
remānsī	I stayed	vīxeram	I had lived	vīcerō	I shall have conquered
remānsistī	you stayed	vīxerās	you had lived	vīceris	you will have conquered
remānsit	he/she/it stayed	vīxerat	he/she/it had lived	vīcerit	he/she/it will have conquered
remānsimus	we stayed	vīxerāmus	we had lived	vīcerimus	we shall have conquered
remānsistis	you stayed	vīxerātis	you had lived	vīceritis	you will have conquered
remānsērun	they stayed	vīxerant	they had lived	vīcerint	they will have conquered

DRILL

A. a. I had said
   b. we shall have sent
   c. you came
   d. they had conquered
   e. they called
   f. fūgērunt
   g. docuerimus
   h. habuerat
   i. vīdistis
   j. sēnseram

B. a. Remānsit   He/she/it remained/stayed a long time in Asia.
   b. mīserint   The gods will have sent her to heaven.
   c. dederat   Caesar had granted/given the king (his) freedom.
   d. scrīpsimus   We wrote/composed a letter about nature.
   e. vīderās   You had seen your son for a long time.

C. a. Nātūram vīcērunt.
   b. Nihil dīxerātis.
   c. Senectūtem vīcerimus.
   d. Multam virtutem sēnsit.
   e. Īnsidiīs cīvitātem suam/eius conservāverat.

PRACTICE SENTENCES

a. These men stayed (stay; will stay; had stayed).
b. The kings conquered (will conquer; conquer; had conquered) Asia.
c. Caesar had come (came; comes; will come) to the same country/area.
d. Caesar said (says; had said; will say) the same things.
e. You gave (will give; had given) us peace.
f. He/she/it had lived (lived; will live) a long time.
g. You had made/done (will make/do; made/did; make/do) it well.
h. They found (had found; will find) him in the same place.
i. God had given (gave; gives; will give) men freedom.
j. You were (used to be; are; will be; had been) free men.

CHAPTER 13

GRAMMAR

1. (subject)
2. (nominative)
3. a. to/for me/myself
   b. to/for/by/with/from you/yourselves
   c. we   us   ourselves
   d. of me/myself (partitive & objective only)
   e. himself   herself   itself   themselves
      by/with/from himself/herself/itself/themselves
   f. you   yourselves
   g. you   yourself
      by/with/from you/yourself
   h. of himself/herself/itself/themselves (objective only)
   i. of you/yourselves(partitive & objective only)
   j. to/for you/yourself
   k. to/for/by/with/from us/ourselves
   l. of us/ourselves (partitive & objective only)
   m. of you/yourself (partitive & objective only)
   n. me   myself
      by/with/from me/myself
   o. to/for himself/herself/itself/themselves

4. ipse   himself   ipsa   herself   ipsum   itself
   ipsīus   ipsīus   ipsīus
   ipsī   ipsī   ipsī
   ipsum   ipsam   ipsum
   ipsō   ipsā   ipsō
   ipsī   themselves   ipsae   themselves ipsa   themselves
   ipsorum   ipsārum   ipsōrum
   ipsīs   ipsīs   ipsīs
   ipsōs   ipsās   ipsa
   ipsīs   ipsīs   ipsīs

The above can also mean myself/yourself/ourselves/yourselves when they modify first or second person pronouns.

5. meus, a, um   tuus, a, um   noster, ra, rum   vester,ra,rum

6. suus, a, um   eius   eōrum   eārum

DRILL

A.   a. suum   He wrote his (own) name.
     b. eius   He/she said/spoke her name.
     c. sibi   The teacher never taught himself wisdom.
     d. eī   The teacher never taught her wisdom.
     e. eius   Before the war, the troops joined/allied themselves with his friends.

B.   a. Virtūtem sibi dedērunt.
     b. Virtūtem eīs dedērunt.
     c. Id mihi dīxī.
     d. Id mihi dīxērunt.
     e. Lībertātem eius cōnservābit.

PRACTICE SENTENCES

a. Cicerō ad Caesarem ipsum vēnit
b. Cicerō se dīlēxit et te dīligis
c. Caesar saved him.
d. Caesar saved himself.
e. The Romans saved themselves.
f. The Romans saved them.
g. The Romans saved him.
h. Caesar saved his (own) friend
i. Caesar saved his friend.

j. They did not save us.
k. We saved ourselves.
l. He/she gave me nothing.
m. I gave myself nothing.
n. He/she gave himself/herself nothing.
o. They gave themselves nothing.
p. I conquered myself.
q. They conquered me.

CHAPTER 14

GRAMMAR

1. (Consonant stems)
2. -is   -es
3. (feminine)
4. -s   -x
5. -e   -al   -ar
6. (genitive plural)
7. [Third (n)]

8. vir	a/the man	vīs	a/the force
virī	of a/the man	vīs	of a/the force
virō	to/for a/the man	vī	to/for a/the force
virum	a/the man	vim	a/the force
virō	by/with/from a/the man	vī	by/with/from a/the force
virī	-/the men	vīres	-/the strength
virōrum	of -/the men	vīrium	of -/the strength
virīs	to/for -/the men	vīribus	to/for -/the strength
virōs	-/the men	vīrēs	-/the strength
virīs	by/with/from -/the men	vīribus	by/with/from -/the strength

 9. (with what?)
10. (how?)
11. (with whom?)
12. (CUM)

13. (no preposition)

14. a. cum cīve   accompaniment
    b. morte   means/instrument
    c. cum sententiā   manner
    d. cum arte   manner
    e. marī   means/instrument
    f. by (the) law   means/instrument
    g. with (the) men   accompaniment
    h. with my eyes   means/instrument
    i. with care   manner
    j. by my work   means/instrument

DRILL

A. a. by/with/from an/the art/skill
    b. to/for/by/with/from a/the sea
    c. of a/the part/share
    d. -/the animals
    e. of the arts/skills
    f. a/the sea
    g. -/the cities
    h. of -/the parts/shares
    i. to/for/by/with/from an/the animal
    j. a/the cloud   -/the clouds

    k. vī
    l. vīrium
    m. cīvium
    n. cum cīvibus
    o. vīribus
    p. maria
    q. mare
    r. cīve
    s. urbī
    t. marī

B. a. urbium   The citizens of the cities are waging wars.
    b. Mare   It restrained/held back the sea.
    c. virtūte   They suffered death with courage.
    d. arte   With skill, you had held the city.
    e. urbem   The king ran across the city.

C. a. Urbem vīribus suis gessit.
    b. Vīs marium eōs/eās/ea tenuit.
    c. Partem sententiārum scrīpsērunt.
    d. Tyrannum trāns urbem trāximus.
    e. Mors animum numquam tenebit.

PRACTICE SENTENCES

a. They themselves had saved the freedom of their own citizens.
b. Part of the citizens ran through the city toward the sea.
c. Magnae sunt vīrēs artium.
d. He himself held the state by force of arms/troops.
e. Those animals have dragged many men into the sea.
f. You dragged him to death across his land.
g. The force of those seas was great.
h. We have derived/inherited/drawn great and beautiful thoughts from ancient men.
i. Cīvis pecūniā (cum cūrā cum amīcīs suis) id fēcit.
j. He waged many wars with the Romans.
k. They governed the state with great wisdom.
l. You said this with great skill.
m. We ran across the city with care.
n. He/she came to us with a large group of citizens.
o. He will overrule the laws of the citizens by force.

CHAPTER 15

GRAMMAR

1. present   imperfect tense   present personal
2. tense   e   third
3. single   snapshot   I led   I have led   I did lead
4. continuing   repeated   habitual   movie
   I was leading   I used ot lead   I kept leading/I habitually led/I repeatedly led
5. (not translated)

6.

timē	b	ō	I shall fear	timē	ba	m	I feared/I was fearing/I used to fear
timē	bi	s	you will fear	timē	bā	s	you feared
timē	bi	t	he/she/it will fear	timē	ba	t	he/she/it feared
timē	bi	mus	we shall fear	timē	bā	mus	we feared
timē	bi	tis	you will fear	timē	bā	tis	you feared
timē	bu	nt	they will fear	timē	ba	nt	they feared
mitt	a	m	I shall send	mittē	ba	m	I sent/I was sending/I used to send
mitt	ē	s	you will send	mittē	bā	s	you sent
mitt	ē	t	he/she/ it will send	mittē	ba	t	he/she/it sent
mitt	ē	mus	we shall send	mittē	bā	mus	we sent
mitt	ē	tis	you will send	mittē	ba	tis	you sent
mitt	ē	nt	they will send	mittē	bu	nt	they sent

7. a. cum puellīs   accompaniment
   b. litterīs   means/instrument
   c. magnā cum virtūte/magnā virtūte   manner
   d. cum virtūte   manner
   e. ūnā hōrā   time
   f. eōdem tempore   time
   g. paucīs hōrīs   time
   h. illō tempore/eō tempore   time
   i. cōpiīs   means/instrument
   j. pecūniā   means/instrument

DRILL

A. a. audēbāmus
   b. iēcit/iaciēbat
   c. cēpit
   d. scribēbam
   e. intellegēbāmus
   f. vēnērunt/veniēbant
   g. audiēbam
   h. mutāvistis
   i. timuērunt
   j. fugiēbās
   k. veniēbant
   l. timēbant
   m. audēbāmus
   n. fūgistī/fugiēbās
   o. iaciēbat
   p. capiēbat
   q. audīvī/audiēbam
   r. scrīpsī/scrībēbam
   s. intelleximus/intellegēbāmus
   t. mūtabātis

B. a. exspectābat   And so the father was expecting his daughter.
   b. mutābunt   Among the citizens, many will change their opinionsminds.
   c. Intellēxistisne   Did you understand the laws?
   d. committēbant   They weree entrusting Italy to (their) fathers.
   e. timēbunt   Sailors will never fear the sea.

C. a. Tyrannum ēiēcērunt.
   b. Cōpiīs partem urbis committēbas/committēbātis.
   c. Pater tuus/vester sententiam eōrum intellēxit.
   d. In mare litterās eius iaciēbāmus.
   e. Philosophia mōrēs eōrum mūtābat.

PRACTICE SENTENCES

a. That tyrant always used to praise himself.
b. I used to come/was coming into the city with my friend.
c. You used to wage/were waging great wars with courage.
d. And so, the Romans conquered the Greeks.
e. Did (Didn't) you see my father at that time?
f. Where did you find this money?
g. They came, and he was telling us the same thing.
h. I never understood/used to understand his books.
i. We never changed our lives.
j. The Romans used to praise the customs of ancient times.

CHAPTER 16

GRAMMAR

1. (I-stem)
2. (two)
3. -ī
4. cīvis, cīvis, m. or f.   mare, maris, n.
5. ablative   genitive

6. potēns	potēns	potēns
potentis	potentis	potentis
potentī	potentī	potentī
potentem	potentem	potēns
potentī	potentī	potentī
potentēs	potentēs	potentia
potentium	potentium	potentium
potentibus	potentibus	potentibus
potentēs	potentēs	potentia
potentibus	potentibus	potentibus
omnis	omnis	omne
omnis	omnis	omnis
omnī	omnī	omnī
omnem	omnem	omne
omnī	omnī	omnī
omnēs	omnēs	omnia
omnium	omnium	omnium
omnibus	omnibus	omnibus
omnēs	omnēs	omnia
omnibus	omnibus	omnibus
celer	celeris	celere
celeris	celeris	celeris

celerī	celerī	celerī
celerem	celerem	celere
celerī	celerī	celerī
celerēs	celerēs	celeria
celerium	celerium	celerium
celeribus	celeribus	celeribus
celerēs	celerēs	celeria
celeribus	celeribus	celeribus

7. yes

DRILL

A. a. to/for/by/with/from every sea
   b. of all (the) parts
   c. all (the) names
   d. to/for a sweet mother
   e. by/with/from every good art/skill
   f. to/for a happy mother
   g. of all (the) wars
   h. to/for a happy man
   i. all (the) seas
   j. by/with/from a sweet girl

   k. by/with/from a sweet mother
   l. all (the) wars
   m. by/with/from a happy man
   n. to/for every good art/skill
   o. to/for a sweet girl
   p. by/with/from a rapid force
   q. by/with/from every part
   r. of every good art/skill
   s. of all (the) kings
   t. by/with/from a happy mother

B. a. Dulcēs — Sweet memories help old age.
   b. brevem — Mothers will always fear a short life.
   c. celeres — How rapid/swift lives are.
   d. miserōs — ācrium — The father helped his bitter sons wretched friends.
   e. fortī — We often used to conquer with a strong body.

C. a. Omnia iūra non sunt bona iūra.
   b. Memoriās vītae difficilis tenuimus.
   c. Brevī aetate bellum mūtāverat.
   d. Unā hōrā omnem amīcum exspectāvistī/exspectāvistīs
   e. De virtūte dulcis fēminae vīrēs trāxērunt.

PRACTICE SENTENCES

a. A long life is often (a) difficult (one).
b. A difficult life can be (a) happy (one).
c. How short was his/her sweet/pleasant life!
d. The memory of an agreeable life pleases/assists/sustains all men.
e. In every land you will see many strong men.
f. That short war was difficult/tough/hard.
g. We overcame all the dangers in a few hours.
h. In a short time he will alter all the citizens' rights.
i. They did not understand the difficult art of sweet liberty.
j. Men fear difficult duties/tasks in all nations/countries.

CHAPTER 17

GRAMMAR

1. relates   refers back   antecedent
2. (complex)
3. (subordinate)
4. to go/fall before

5. (function of its clause)
6. (antecedent)

7.

quī	who	quae	who	quod	which
cuius	of whom/whose	cuius	of whom/whose	cuius	of which/whose
cui	to/for whom	cui	to/for whom	cui	to/for which
quem	whom	quam	whom	quod	which
quō	by/with/from whom	quā	by/with/from whom	quō	by/with/from which
quī	who	quae	who	quae	which
quōrum	of whom/whose	quārum	of whom/whose	quōrum	of which/whose
quibus	to/for whom	quibus	to/for whom	quibus	to/for which
quōs	whom	quās	whom	quae	which
quibus	by/with/ from whom	quibus	by/with/ from whom	quibus	by/with/ from which

DRILL

A. a. the boy whose book
 b. the eyes which
 c. the strength by which
 d. the letter which
 e. that which
 f. that/this woman with whom
 g. the citizens who
 h. the law by which
 i. the city through which
 j. the place which

k. cīvitās quam
l. fīliam cuius
m. maria trāns quae
n. librī in quibus
o. fēmina cui
p. cīvem quī
q. amīcōs quibuscum
r. litterae quae
s. fīliī quōs
t. puellās quae

B. a. quam
 b. quō
 c. cuius
 d. quae
 e. quās

The truth which you told was difficult.
The deed by which we conquered was great.
I had seen the woman whose son had fled.
We feel a friendship which will not change itself.
The roads across which they were running were long.

C. a. Insidae quās timuimus malae sunt.
 b. Illās cōpiās quibuscum vēnistī/vēnistīs dūcēs/dūcētis.
 c. Amīcitiam quam habēmus dēlebit.
 d. Hominem/virum cuius facta magna erant neglēxērunt.
 e. Aetās quae incipit beāta erit.

PRACTICE SENTENCES

a. They praised the citizens whom you had sent.
b. They praised the citizen who had saved the country.
c. They praised the citizen whose son had saved the country.
d. They praised the citizens whose sons had saved the country.
e. They praised the citizen to whom they had entrusted the country.
f. They praised the citizens to whom they had entrusted the country.
g. The tyrant destroyed the cities from which the citizens had fled.
h. The tyrant destroyed the cities into which the citizens had fled.
i. He gave the books to the girls whom he was praising.
j. He entrusted his life to the man whose daughter you love.

CHAPTER 18

GRAMMAR

1. (subject)
2. (object)
3. (object)
4. (subject)
5. a. The player   b. by the player
6. a. his opponent   b. The opponent
7. laudārī   monērī   to be praised   to be warned
8. r

9. iuvor   I am helped   iuvābor   I shall be helped   iuvābar I used to be helped
    I am being helped
iuvāris you are helped   iuvāberis you will be helped   iuvābāris you used to be helped
iuvātur he/she/it is helped   iuvābitur he/she/it will be helped iuvābātur he/she/it used to be helped
iuvāmur we are helped   iuvābimur we shall be helped   iuvābāmur we used to be helped
iuvāminī you are helped   iuvābiminī you will be helped   iuvābāminī you used to be helped
iuvāntur they are helped   iuvābuntur they will be helped   iuvābantur they used to be helped

10. deleor I am destroyed   delēbor I shall be destroyed   delēbar I used to be destroyed
    I am being destroyed
delēris you are destroyed   delēberis you will be destroyed   delēbāris you used to be destroyed
delētur he/she/it is destroyed delēbitur he/she/it will be destroyed delēbātur he/she/it used to be destroyed
delēmur we are destroyed   delēbimur we shall be destroyed   delēbāmur we used to be destroyed
delēminī you are destroyed   delēbiminī you will be destroyed delēbāminī you used to be destroyed
delēntur they are destroyed   delēbuntur they will be destroyed delēbantur they used to be destroyed

11. a. none   things/ideas
    b. cum   people
    c. optional/cum   ideas
    d. none   nouns of time
    e. ab(a)   people

DRILL

A. a. you will be called
   b. you were being/used to be called
   c. you are/are being called
   d. they used to be/were being taught
   e. they are/are being taught
   f. they will be taught
   g. we shall be changed
   h. we used to be/were being changed
   i. you used to be/were being held
   j. you will be held

   k. timēbātur
   l. timētur
   m. timēbitur
   n. exspectābor
   o. exspector
   p. exspectābar
   q. vidēbāmur
   r. vidēbimur
   s. tolerātur
   t. tolerābitur

B. a. docentur   In school, the girls are being taught.
   b. movēbuntur   The boys will not be influenced/affected by the teacher
   c. delēbantur   All the cities were being destroyed by the troops.
   d. exspectābātur A delay of plans was being anticipated by us.
   e. servābimur   We shall be saved by these types of treachery.

C. a. Lūdus hōc cōnsiliō mutābitur.
   b. Istō genere lūdi non adiuvābāmur.
   c. Etiam a patre suō nōn movētur.

d. A tuis/vestris cīvibus non timēberis/timēbiminī.

e. Litterae a fīliā meā tenēbantur.

PRACTICE SENTENCES

a. They frighten me; I am (being) frightened by them; I am (being) frightened by their force.

b. He was being influenced by friends; he was being influenced by their plans.

c. We are not destroyed by the strength of men, but we can be destroyed by treachery.

d. You yourself are not changed, but your name is changed.

e. Books of this kind were being given to the boys by the teacher.

f. Freedom will be given to the people by the king in a short time.

g. Our nation can even now be saved by strong citizens.

h. We must be warned by the fate of others.

i. We shall be assisted by powerful friends.

j. We praise all our men who are motivated by courage and truth, not by self-esteem.

CHAPTER 19

GRAMMAR

1. perfect participle   present
2. perfect participle   imperfect
3. perfect participle   future

4. amor - I am loved/am being loved
   amāris - you are loved/are being loved
   amātur - he/she/it is loved/is being loved
   amāmur - we are loved/are being loved
   amāminī - you are loved/are being loved
   amantur - they are loved/are being loved

   amātus, a sum - I was loved/have been loved
   amātus, a es - you were loved/have been loved
   amātus, a, um est - he/she/it was loved/has been loved
   amātī, ae sumus - we were loved/have been loved
   amātī, ae estis - you were loved/have been loved
   amātī, ae, a sunt - they were loved/have been loved

5. terrēbar - I was being/used to be frightened
   terrēbāris - you were being/used to be frightened
   terrēbātur - he/she/it was being/used to be frightened
   terrēbāmur - we were being/used to be frightened
   terrēbāminī - you were being/used to be frightened
   terrēbantur - they were being/used to be frightened

   terrītus, a eram - I had been frightened
   terrītus, a erās - you had been frightened
   terrītus, a, um erat - he/she/it had been frightened
   terrītī, ae erāmus - we had been frightened
   terrītī, ae erātis - you had been frightened
   terrītī, ae, a erant - they had been frightened

6. missus, a erō   I shall have been sent
   missus, a eris   you will have been sent
   missus, a, um erit   he/she/it will have been sent
   missī, ae erimus   we shall have been sent
   missī, ae eritis   you will have been sent
   missī, ae, a erunt   they will have been sent

7. relative			
8. nominative	accusative (feminine)	ablative (feminine)	accusative (neuter)
9. interrogative	relative		
10. interrogative	interrogative	relative	
11. no	has not	yes	yes
yes	has not	yes	yes
no	has	no	not always

12. quis? - who? -
   cuius? - of whom?/whose?
   cui? - to/for whom?
   quem? - whom?

   quis? - who?
   cuius? - of whom?whose?
   cui? - to/for whom?
   quem? - whom?

   quid? - what?
   cuius? - of what?/whose?
   cui? - to/for what?
   quid? - what?

quō? - by/with/from whom?

qui? - what?/which?

cuius? - of what?/which?

cui? - to/for what?/which?

quem? - what?/which?

quō? - by/with/from what?/which?

quo? - by/with/from whom?

quae? - what?/which?

cuius? - of what?/which?

cui? - to/for what?/which?

quam? - what?/which?

quā? - by/with/from what?/which?

quō? - by/with/from what?

quod? /what?/which?

cuius? - of what?/which?

cui? - to/for what?/which?

quod? - what?/which?

quō? - by/with/from what?/which?

13. quī? - who? (what?/which?)

quōrum? - of whom?/whose?

quibus? - to/for whom?

quos? - whom?

quibus? - by/with/from whom?

quae? - who?

quārum? of whom?/whose?

quibus? to/for whom?

quās? - whom?

quibus? - by/with/from whom?

quae? - what?

quōrum?- of what?/whose?

quibus? - to/for what?

quae? - what?

quibus?- by/with/from what?

DRILL

A.

1. a. I lead, I am leading, I do lead
   b. I am led, I am being led
   c. I led, I have led, I did lead
   d. I was led, I have been led
   e. I was leading, I used to lead, I habitually led
   f. I was being led, I used to be led, I was habitually led
   g. I had led
   h. I shall lead
   i. I shall have led
   j. I shall have been led
   k. captī, ae sumus
   l. capiebamus
   m. capiemus
   n. ceperimus
   o. captī, ae erimus

2. a. of whom?/whose?   of which ones?   of what women?   of which women?
   b. who?   which one?
   c. of whom/whose/of which
   d. what?   which one?
   e. which
   f. whom
   g. whom?   which one?   what/which man?   what/which woman?
   h. by/with/from whom
   i. by/with/from whom?/which one?   by/with/from what/which man/woman?
   j. cuius
   k. quis?
   l. quid?
   m. quem?
   n. quem
   o. quod

B. a. datum erat — In/within an hour, the judgment/opinion had been rendered/given.
   b. quibus ēiectī estis — By whom/which ones were you thrown out?
   c. dēlētī erimus — In/within a short time, we shall have been destroyed.
   d. Quōrum parātum est — Whose judgment/opinion has been prepared?
   e. quō līberatī erant — By whom had they been freed?

C. a. Senex neglēctus erat.
   b. Quō novō lūdō iutī/adiūtī erant?
   c. Quā hōrā/Quō tempore servāta erit?
   d. Ab eō diū neglēctī erāmus.
   e. Quō nōmine tum vocātus, a es/vocātī, ae estis?

PRACTICE SENTENCES

a. The teacher by whom the book was prepared is overloaded with work.
b. I myself saw the boy who was saved.

c. I never saw the old man whose sons were saved.

d. Peace and freedom were praised by the citizen who had been sent.

e. Friendship was praised by the citizens who had been sent.

f. To whom was the book given? (was the book being given?) (had the book been given?)

g. What was said to the boy to whom the book was given?

h. Who/Which one was saved? What/which boy was saved?

i. Whose sons were saved?

j. Who/Which one was sent?

k. Whom/Which ones did you see in the city?

l. What things were found there by you?

m. By whom was this said?

n. Whose sons were praised by him?

o. What danger frightens you?

CHAPTER 20

GRAMMAR

1. u
2. dative plural   ablative plural
3. masculine
4. manus   masculine
5. (rare)
6. motion   ab(a)   de   ex(e)
7. (no preposition)
8. (optional preposition)
9. (always preposition)

10.

	a/the fear		a/the horn
metūs	of a/the fear	cornūs	of a/the horn
metuī	to/for a/the fear	cornū	to/for a/the horn
metum	a/the fear	cornū	a/the horn
metū	by/with/from a the fear	cornū	by/with/from a/the horn
metūs	the fears	cornua	-/the horns
metuum	of the fears	cornuum	of the horns
metibus	to/for the fears	cornibus	to/for the horns
metūs	-/the fears	cornua	-/the horns
metibus	by/with/from the fears	cornibus	by/with/from the horns

DRILL

A. a. to/for the senate
   b. by/with/from a verse
   c. of the fears
   d. the hands/bands
   e. the senate
   f. to/for/by/with/from fears/anxieties
   g. -/the verses
   h. to/for the hand/band
   i. by/with/from a/the fear/anxiety
   j. a/the hand/band

   k. senātūs
   l. manuī
   m. frūctus
   n. versibus
   o. cornua
   p. metūs
   q. manibus
   r. frūctūs
   s. senātū
   t. metus

B. a. metum
   b. frūctibus metibus
   c. manūs servitūte

We overcame the fear of slavery in Greece.
You lacked neither enjoyments nor anxieties.
These bands had been freed from slavery.

d. manū metū
e. senātum

C. a. Metus sceleris populum terruit.
   b. In Graeciā, frūctūs servitūtis intellēctī sunt.
   c. Gravēs versūs a fīliō meō scrīptī erant.
   d. Lēgēs/iūra contrā scelus cīvēs servant.
   e. Commūnī amicītiā populī caret.

Within the group, the friends lacked fear.
The judgment was rendered by the king against the senate.

PRACTICE SENTENCES

a. Who came to us at that time?
b. What was said by him?
c. We freed them from the crimes of that tyrant.
d. They now are free from every fear.
e. Their sons are reading good books in our schools with eagerness.
f. These verses thank us profusely.
g. For/Therefore those poor people now enjoy/have the fruits/benefits of peace and freedom without fear.
h. Good men will never be deprived of an abundance of these benefits/fruits.

CHAPTER 21

GRAMMAR

1. parāre   movēre   mittere   ēicere   invenīre
   parārī   movērī   mittī   ēicī   invenīrī

2. mittō   mittor   ēiciō   ēicior   inveniō   invenior
   mittis   mitteris   ēicis   ēiceris   invenīs   invenīris
   mittit   mittitur   ēicit   ēicitur   invenit   invenitur
   mittimus   mittimur   ēicimus   ēicimur   invenīmus   invenīmur
   mittitis   mittiminī   ēicitis   ēiciminī   invenītis   invenīminī
   mittunt   mittuntur   ēiciunt   ēiciuntur   inveniunt   inveniuntur

3. mittam   mittar
   mittēs   mittēris
   mittet   mittētur
   mittēmus   mittēmur
   mittētis   mittēminī
   mittent   mittentur
   ēiciam   ēiciar
   ēiciēs   ēiciēris
   ēiciet   ēiciētur
   ēiciēmus   ēiciēmur
   ēiciētis   ēiciēminī
   ēicient   ēicientur
   inveniam   inveniar
   inveniēs   inveniēris
   inveniet   inveniētur
   inveniēmus   inveniēmur
   inveniētis   inveniēminī
   invenient   invenientur

4.   mittēbam   mittēbar
                mittēbās   mittēbāris

mittēbat	mittēbātur
mittēbāmus	mittēbāmur
mittēbātis	mittēbāminī
mittēbant	mittēbantur
ēiciēbam	ēiciēbar
ēiciēbās	ēiciēbāris
ēiciēbat	ēiciēbātur
ēiciēbāmus	ēiciēbāmur
ēiciēbātis	ēiciēbāminī
ēiciebant	ēiciēbantur
inveniēbam	inveniēbar
inveniēbās	inveniēbāris
inveniēbat	inveniēbātur
inveniēbāmus	inveniēbāmur
inveniēbātis	inveniēbāminī
inveniēbant	inveniēbantur

DRILL

A. a. You will be conquered
   b. He/she/it is known
   c. We shall be ordered
   d. They were being/used to be seized
   e. I was being/used to be restrained
   f. You will be known
   g. I shall be seized
   h. I shall be restrained
   i. you are known
   j. you will be known

   k. iubēbat
   l. rapiēbantur/raptī sunt
   m. continēbitur
   n. iubeō
   o. raptī
   p. continēbuntur
   q. rapiēbāmur
   r. sciētur
   s. vincō
   t. vincor

B. a. scitur   The cause/reason is known.
   b. continēbimur   We shall be restrained/contained within the boundaries/territory.
   c. scribēbantur   The verses werewere being/used to be written for the sake of praise.
   d. iubentur   The peoples/nations of the world are commanded by me.
   e. sciēminī   By your courage, you will be known.

C. a. Gentis causā iubēbitur.
   b. Fīnēs rapiēbantur.
   c. Litterās saepe scribēbāmus.
   d. Fīnēs bene sciuntur.
   e. Gēns numquam continēbitur.

PRACTICE SENTENCES

a. Who is sent (will be sent; used to be sent; was sent)?
b. By whom will this letter be sent (was this letter sent; is this letter sent)?
c. What was said (used to be said; will be said; is said)?
d. You will be neglected (were neglected) for a long time.
e. For the sake of the state, they ordered him to be captured.
f. His spirit/soul was not able to/could not be touched/reached by money.
g. Love of country was being felt (will be felt; is felt; was felt) in every soul.
h. Throughby love of country we are united (used to be united; will be united) with other citizens.
i. Wisdom and truth will not be found (are not found; were not found) in foolish men.
j. Wisdom is not acquired (will not be acquired; was not acquired) even with/by much money.

CHAPTER 22

GRAMMAR

1. e
2. feminine
3. diēs   masculine

4.

fideī	a/the faith	fidēs	the faiths
fideī	of a/the faith	fidērum	of the faiths
fidem	to/for a/the faith	fidēbus	to/for the faiths
fidem	a/the faith	fidēs	-the faiths
fidē	by/with/from a/the faith	fidēbus	by/with/from the faiths

5. 1. Means/instrument   (thing, idea)
   2. Accompaniment   cum (people)
   3. Manner   cum (optional w/adj)   cum
   4. Time when/within which (nouns of time)
   5. Personal agent   ab (person)
   6. Place from which   ab/de/ex (motion)
   7. Separation   (verbs = to free   (other verbs with thing)   ab/de/ex
                       to lack   (other verbs w/person)
                       to deprive)
   8. Place where   in (nouns of place)

DRILL

A. a. of the things
    b. to/for/by/with/from the days (time)
    c. to/for hope
    d. a/the faith
    e. a/the hope
    f. by/with/from the republic
    g. by/with/from the day (time)
    h. -/the hopes
    i. of the faith
    j. -/the days

    k. reī pūblicae
    l. (cum) spē (manner)
    m. illō diē (time)
    n. fīdeī
    o. multīs diēbus
    p. rem
    q. spēs incerta
    r. novās rēs/nova
    s. ūnō diē
    t. spērum

B. a. He/she/it remained in the city.   place where
    b. He/she/it will come in anone hour.   time when/within which
    c. He/she/it came at that time.   time when/within which
    d. He/she/it came with them.   accompaniment
    e. He/she/it came from the city.   place from which
    f. They lack fire.   separation
    g. That was accomplished by fire.   means/instrument
    h. That was accomplished by them.   personal agent
    i. That was accomplished with faith.   manner

C. a. Fidēs   The faith of nations is strong.
    b. Spēs   The hope of peace will never be taken away/removed/destroyed.
    c. fidē   The fire of the soul is sustained by faith.
    d. reī publicae Many citizens of the republic are being rescued.
    e. diērum   The number of days is uncertain.

PRACTICE SENTENCES

a. He ruled the republic with great care.
b. (On) that day, they prepared many things with hope.
c. In a few days, Cicero will rescue the republic from danger.
d. You freed all the republics from fear.
e. The earth nourishes/sustains men with good products/fruits.

CHAPTER 23

GRAMMAR

1. (four)
2. two present & future
3. two perfect & future

4. active	present	-ns, ntis	
passive	future	(-nd)us, a, um	
5. passive	perfect	-us, a, um	
active	future	(-ur)us, a, um	

6. mūtāns, ntis	changing		being changed
	having changed	mūtatus, a, um	having been changed
mūtātūrus, a, um	about to change	mūtandus, a, um	needing to be changed
docēns, ntis	teaching		being taught
	having taught	doctus, a, um	having been taught
doctūrus, a, um	about to teach	docendus, a, um	needing to be taught
legēns, ntis	reading/choosing		being read/chosen
	having read/chosen	lēctus, a, um	having been read/chosen
lēctūrus, a, um	about to read/choose	legendus, a, um	needing to be read/chosen
rapiēns, ntis	stealing		being stolen
	having stolen	raptus, a, um	having been stolen
raptūrus, a, um	about to steal	rapiendus, a, um	needing to be stolen
sentiēns, ntis	feeling		being felt
	having felt	sēnsus, a, um	having been felt
sēnsūrus, a, um	about to feel	sentiendus, a, um	needing to be felt

7. about to   going to
8. having to be   needing to be
9. potēns, potentis   magnus, a, um
10. main   absolute   contemporaneous   prior   subsequent
11. (clauses or phrases fitting context)

DRILL

A. a. about to press
   b. pressing
   c. about to desire/want
   d. about to give
   e. needing to be pressed
   f. having been desired
   g. needing to be given
   h. needing to be desired
   i. having been pressed
   j. desiring

k. vīsus, a, um
l. scrīptūrus, a, um
m. scrībēns, ntis
n. videndus, a, um
o. scrībendus, a, um
p. mittendus, a, um
q. vidēns, ntis
r. scrīptus, a, um
s. missūrus, a, um
t. visūrus, a, um

B. a. inventus   The speaker who was found is not able to speak.
  b. dāns   When he gave the signal, he ran.
  c. oppressūri   We ourselves, as we were about to overrun the city, heard the speaker's advice.
  d. cupīta   He stole the coveted gifts.
  e. vidēns   When he sees the signs, the king will understand.

C. a. Dōna ostenta missa sunt.
  b. Iūcunda sōla cupiēntes beāti umquam erimus?
  c. Senātus lēgem mūtātūrus gentem/populum timuit.
  d. Urbs opprimenda igne superāta est.
  e. Iūcunda petēntes fīdem neglēximus.

PRACTICE SENTENCES

a. After he was/had been captured, he said nothing.
b. He thanked those who were giving gifts.
c. I do not like someone who seeks gifts.
d. I sent my son to your school because he needed to be educated.
e. Because we are frightened by this plot, we shall lead a wretched life.
f. Those unfortunate men, since they were seen by the tyrant, ran across the border.
g. We fear someone who fears us.
h. The old man, after he was warned by friends, fled to us.
i. Who, once freed from these dangers, will not thank the gods.
j. Nothing is doubtful for those who have faith.

CHAPTER 24

GRAMMAR

1. participle	ablative	ablative absolute
2. loosely connected	commas	
3. subject	object	
4. ablative	present participle	
5. conjunction		
6. because	when	since	if	although
7. debere	infinitive	personal agent
8. esse	passive periphrastic	
9. predicate adjective	gender	number	case	subject
10. personal agent	dative	agent

DRILL

A. a. Servō captō   After the slave had been captured, the generals recaptured the city.
  b. quaerendum   Power must be sought by the general;.
  c. Lībertāte receptā   Once freedom had been regained, the slaves sought peace.
  d. expellendī   The evil men must be exiled by the leader.
  e. Spē relictā   Once hope had been abandoned, each one fled.

B. a. Hīs dictīs/Hīs rēbus dictīs, dux dōna accēpit.
  b. Illud/Istud signum tibi/vōbīs dandum est.
  c. Rēge expulsō, senātus iūra/lēgēs fēcit.
  d. Hī versūs poētae scrībendī sunt.
  e. Cūr imperium cuique relinquendum erat/fuit?

PRACTICE SENTENCES

a. When good men hold the power, The republic will be strong/flourish/prosper.
b. When every desire for money and glory had been expunged/banished from his soul, that leader/commander conquered himself.
c. All the citizens used to fear that tyrant who had to be exiled.
d. When the dictator had been conquered, the citizens regained freedom and rights.
e. When many nations had been conquered, you wanted to possess the entire world.
f. Slavery of every kind must be eliminated through the entire world.
g. All rights therefore must be protected by the citizens with great care.
h. Once the positions have been surrendered by the citizens, the republic will be in great danger.
i. Truth and courage must always be sought by all men.
j. Once truth and courage had been sought, the republic was saved.

CHAPTER 25

GRAMMAR

1. e ī
2. perfect third -isse
3. perfect passive esse future active esse
4. (no)

5.
nārrāre	to tell	nārrārī	to be told
nārrāvisse	to have told	nārrātum, am, um esse	to have been told
nārrātūrum, am, um esse	to be about to tell		to be about to be told
terrēre	to frighten	terrērī	to be frightened
terruisse	to have frightened	territum, am, um esse	to have been frightened
territūrum, am, um esse	to be about to frighten		to be about to be frightened
expellere	to banish	expellī	to be banished
expulisse	to have banished	expulsum, am, um esse	to have been banished
expulsūrum, am, um esse	to be about to banish		to be about to be banished
accipere	to receive	accipī	to be received
accēpisse	to have received	acceptum, am, um esse	to have been received
acceptūrum, am, um esse	to be about to receive		to be about to be received
scīre	to know	scīrī	to be known
scīvisse	to have known	scītum, am, um esse	to have been known
scītūrum, am, um esse	to be about to know		to be about to be known

6. predicate adjectives subject
7. quotation
8. saying knowing thinking perceiving
9. a. dīcō d. nārrō
   b. negō e. scrībō
   c. nūntiō f. ostendō
10. a. sciō c. intellegō
    b. nesciō d. memoriā teneō
11. a. crēdō c. spērō
    b. putō
12. a. audiō c. sentiō
    b. videō
13. (b)
14. accusative reflexive regular

15.   tense   time
16. a. amāvisse
    b. amāre
    c. amātūrum esse

DRILL

A. a. I see   f.
   b. I deny   g. I show
   c.   h. I hope
   d. I believe   i.
   e.   j. I think
   f. vīsās esse

B. a. to be moved
   b. to have believed   g. mūtātūrum/versūrum esse
   c. to have been drawn/dragged   h. scīrī
   d. to be said   i. tetigisse
   e. to have supported/carried   j. quaesītum esse

C. a. esse   He denied that the young man was his son.
   b. relictūrum esse   I believe that I will relinquish/give up power.
   c. vēnisse   The senate announced that the enemy had come.
   d. captōs esse   The slaves will say that they were captured here.
   e. darī   We shall see that gifts are given/donated.

D. a. Sciō eum ventūrum esse.
   b. Crēdidērunt eum dōna mīsisse.
   c. Vidēbitis lūdum parārī.
   d. Populus/Gēns nārrāvit sē monitum/monitam esse.
   e. Crēdimus animum hūmānum immortālem esse.

PRACTICE SENTENCES

a. They hope that you will see him.
b. I know that this was/has been done by you.
c. I did not know that those things had been done by him.
d. They used to think that the tyrant had to be exiled by them.
e. We believe that peace must be sought by all leaders.
f. Our enemies believe that the entire republic must be conquered by them.
g. The enemy hopes that he will conquer all the republics.
h. I know well that do not know many things no one can truly know all things.

CHAPTER 26

GRAMMAR

1. clear/bright   famous/illustrious
2. clarior, clarius   clearer/more clear/too clear/rather clear
3. two-ending   third   consonant
   ablative singular   genitive plural   nominative & accusative neuter plural
4. vowel
5. than   the same case
6. clārissimus, a, um   clearest/most clear/very clear
7. magnus, a, um
8. vowel
9. as strong as possible
10. potentior, ius   potentissimus, a, um
    iūcundior, ius   iūcundissimus, a, um

magis perpetuus, a, um	maximē perpetuus, a, um
dulcior, ius	dulcissimus, a, um
sapientior, ius	sapientissimus, a, um

DRILL

A. a. more/too/rather pleasant/agreeable
   b. most heavy/serious/important/heaviest/very heavy
   c. by/with/from the shorter/too short/shorter/briefer
   d. more/too/rather ugly/shameful/disgraceful/uglier
   e. of the more/too/rather difficult
   f. to/for the most/very uncertain
   g. more/too/rather common/general
   h. to/for the more/too/rather suitable
   i. of the most/very loyal/faithful
   j. of the more/too/rather true/real

   k. breviōrem
   l. quam longissimī
   m. beātius/fēlīcius
   n. maximē idōnea
   o. incertissimō
   p. acerbiōribus
   q. gravius
   r. dulcissimārum
   s. cāriōrum
   t. sapientiōre

B. a. potentiōrem — Avoid the more powerful light.
   b. acerbissimōs — The author wrote/composed the harshest/most bitter verses.
   c. clārissimae — The memory of the brightest light remained.
   d. fidēliōrem — I believe that she is more loyal than he (is).
   e. brevissimās — The enemy will send the shortest letter possible/ as short a letter as possible.

C. a. Mittite quam sapientissimōs hominēs/virōs.
   b. Breviōrem librum legēs/legētis.
   c. Nihi l est certius quam mors.
   d. Perīculum mihi gravius est.
   e. Iūcundissimae memoriae semper remanent.

PRACTICE SENTENCES

a. They announced that as strong a leader/commander as possible had come.
b. When the very bright/brightest light had been seen by everyone/all, the strongest troops weredispatched against the enemy.
c. After that very evil man had been exiled, the senate distributed/donated gifts to the more loyal/faithful citizens.
d. This author is more famous than that one.
e. Certain people said that this author was more famous than that one.
f. Because/Since some/certain very sensible/intelligent books had been read, we avoided those more/too/rather evil vices.
g. Who is the happiest man?
h. The cure for your vices is considered/viewed asseen as more/too/rather difficult.
i. That leader/commander/general felt/estimated that teh nation was dearer to him than life.
j. A band of as loyal/faithful young men/people as possible must be sought by the senate.

CHAPTER 27

GRAMMAR

1. facilis, e (easy) — facilior, ius — facillimus, a, um
   difficilis, e (hard/difficult) — difficilior, ius — difficillimus, a, um
   similis, e (same/similar) — similior, ius — simillimus, a, um
   dissimilis, e (unlike/dissimilar) — dissimilior, ius — dissimillimus, a, um
   humilis, e (low/humble) — humilior, ius — humillimus, a, um
   gracilis, e (slender) — gracilior, ius — gracillimus, a, um

2. līber, era, erum (free) — līberior, ius — līberrimus, a, um
   pulcher, chra, chrum — pulchrior, ius — pulcherrimus, a, um
      (pretty/beautiful)
   ācer, ācris, ācre (keen/bitter) — ācrior, ius — acerrimus, a, um

3. malus, a, um (bad)   peior, peius (worse)   pessimus, a, um (worst)
  prae/prō (before/in front of)   prior, prius (former)   prīmus, a, um (first
  superus, a, um (that above)   superior, ius (higher)   summus, a, um (highest)
                                                     suprēmus, a, um (last)
  parvus, a, um (small)   minor, minus (smaller)   minimus, a, um (smallest)
  magnus, a, um (great)   maior, ius (greater)   maximus, a, um (greatest)
  bonus, a, um (good)   melior, ius (better)   optimus, a, um (best)

4. plūs
  plūris
  plūs
  plūre

5. plūrēs   plūra
  plūrium   plūrium
  plūribus   plūribus
  plūrēs   plūra
  plūribus   plūribus

DRILL

A. a. a larger war
  b. a very similar book
  c. the smallest boy
  d. The prettiest/most beautiful girl
  e. a worse fruit
  f. more work
  g. more jobs/tasks
  h. the first gifts
  i. the worst citizens
  j. more praise

  k. auctor optimus
  l. pulcherrimus sōl
  m. liber difficilior
  n. versus facillimī
  o. labor difficilior
  p. populus līberior
  q. ratiōnēs pessimae
  r. diēs suprēmus
  s. amīcitia maior
  t. caela summa

B. a. optima
  b. Celerrimum   maximum
  c. Sapientiōrēs   minorem
  d. plūs
  e. difficilior

The sun's light is the best.
The fastest cure is not always the greatest.
Wiser men often write a small number of books.
The ancestors/elders were expecting more from the young men.
Old age is a more difficult period/time of life.

C. a. Fīlius eius erat maior quam filia eius.
  b. Filia erat pulchrior quan māter sua.
  c. Maiōrēs nostrī sōlem deum appellābant.
  d. Maximae amīcitiae saepe sunt difficillimae.
  e. Plūrēs auctōrēs de patriā/terrā suā scrībebant.

PRACTICE SENTENCES

a. The easiest things are often not the best.
b. The difficult things are often the greatest.
c. The better studies/courses are the more difficult.
d. The smaller boy took the larger gift.
e. More men believe this war to be worse than the first war.
f. The better general/commander will come with larger reinforcements.
g. They gave greater power and more money to the better commander/leader.
h. The citizens of smaller cities are not better than those of the largest cities.
i. We ourselves are not better than most men of prior eras.
j. Our ancestors used to call Apollo the god of the sun.

CHAPTER 28

GRAMMAR

1. fact/certainty
2. doubt/possibility/wish
3. (rarely)
4. (frequently)
5. e   active   passive   a
6. amem   videam   mittam   rapiar   inveniar
   amēs   videas   mittas   rapiāris   inveniāris
   amet   videat   mittat   rapiātur   inveniātur
   amēmus   videamus   mittamus   rapiāmur   inveniāmur
   ametis   videātis   mittātis   rapiāminī   inveniāminī
   ament   videant   mittant   rapiantur   inveniantur
7. context
8. command
9. hortatory subjunctive   imperative   jussive subjunctive
10. infinitive   subjunctive
11. ut   nē

DRILL

A. a. we are heard/are being heard
   b. 3 pers plur passive
   c. 1 pers sing active
   d. you will be freed
   e. he sends/is sending/does send
   f. they will be known
   g. you will be received
   h. you name/are naming/do name
   i. 2 pers plur passive
   j. we shall be heard
   k. 1 pers plur passive
   l. you are freed/are being freed
   m. you are received/are being received
   n. 2 pers plur passive
   o. they are known/are being known
   p. he/she will send
   q. I will be ordered/1 pers sing passive
   r. I was being ordered/used to be ordered
   s. 2 pers sing passive
   t. 3 pers sing active

B. a. praestēmus   Let us not offer/furnish arms.
   b. dent   Let them give their word for the sake of freedom/cause of liberty.
   c. audiāmus vīvāmus   Let's hear the speaker to live in peacein order that we may live in peace.
   d. timeant   Let us exile the worst citizens in order that the best may not fear treachery.
   e. laudem   Let me praise the advantages of friendship.

C. a. Nōbīs arma mittat.
   b. Veniunt ut meliora arma praestent.
   c. Perīculum bellī vitēmus.
   d. Illa verba scrībit ut populum adiuvet/iuvet.
   e. Litterās legat nē fugiat.

PRACTICE SENTENCES

a. Let that commander come. We are expecting him.
b. He bestows kindnesses on others to be loved.
c. I am telling you these pleasant words in order that you will not leave.
d. For the sake of the nation, let's accomplish these very difficult things.
e. Let's take up arms in order that our freedom not be taken away.
f. Will (Won't) our freedom be rescued from danger by arms alone?
g. Let scholars not write the more difficult books.
h. We shall not really derive wisdom from the more difficult books.
i. Let him accomplish better and bigger things in order that he may not lead a very wretched life.
j. Explain these things to that very famous author in order that they may be written in his book.

CHAPTER 29

GRAMMAR

1. active infinitive present   second   active   passive

2.

appellārer	movērer	vincerer	iacerem	sentīrem
appellārēris	movērēris	vincerēris	iacerēs	sentīrēs
appellārētur	movērētur	vincerētur	iaceret	sentīret
appellārēmur	movērēmur	vincerēmur	iacerēmus	sentīrēmus
appellārēminī	movērēminī	vincerēminī	iacerētis	sentīrētis
appellārentur	movērentur	vincerentur	iacerent	sentīrent

3.

sim	possim	essem	possem
sīs	possīs	essēs	possēs
sit	possit	esset	posset
sīmus	possīmus	essēmus	possēmus
sītis	possītis	essētis	possētis
sint	possint	essent	possent

4. past
5. indicative   imperative   subjunctive
6. ut
7. ne   ut nōn/nēmō/nihil
8.

     tam/ita (adjective/adverb)   so

     sīcita (verb)   so/to such a degree

     tantus, a, um (noun)   so large/so great

DRILL

A. a. 3 pers sing imperfect active
   b. 1 pers plur imperfect active
   c. you will be exiled
   d. 2 pers sing imperfect active
   e. 2 pers plur imperfect active
   f. you will find
   g. we can/are able to
   h. 3 pers sing present active
   i. he says/is saying/does say
   j. They are being moved

   k. 3 pers sing imperfect active
   l. we see/are seeing/do see
   m. 3 pers plur imperfect active
   n. 3 pers plur present active
   o. 1 pers plur present
   p. 2 pers sing present active
   q. you will rescue
   r. 2 pers sing imperfect active
   s. 2 pers plur imperfect passive
   t. 3 pers plur imperfect passive

B. a. discerent   The students read so many books that they learned the truth.
   b. legēremus   The author wrote so well that we read all his books.
   c. habēret   The young man was so unfeeling that he did not have friends.
   d. dārēmus   He said so many things that we gave you the power.
   e. discam   This school is so good that I am learning many things.

C. a. Signum tam clārum erat ut omnēs id vidērent.
   b. Lēgēs/Iūra ita durae/dura sunt ut nulla lībertās sit.
   c. Eōs armīs adiūvit nē urbs vincerētur/superārētur.
   d. Tam bene scrībēbat/scrīpsit ut discipulī versus suōs discerent.
   e. Tantam mentem habēs ut multa discere possīs.

PRACTICE SENTENCES

a. We used to read good books with care to learn wisdom.
b. The best books must be read by the students so that they may learn the truth and good habits.
c. The minds/souls of most men are so foolish that they do not want/desire to learn.
d. But many minds are so sharp/keen that they are able to learn well.

e. Let all citizens devote themselves to the nation in order that the enemy may not destroy freedom.

f. Caesar was such a capable commander that the enemy did not conquer Roman soldiers.

g. You used to bestow such great favors that everyone loved you.

h. He was so unfeeling that no one liked him.

i. Many citizens were fleeing that area to not be persecuted by the tyrant.

j. They loved freedom so much that they were never conquered by the enemy.

CHAPTER 30

GRAMMAR

1. perfect   eri   isse
2. participle   present   imperfect
3. mutāverim   mōverim   trāxissem   iēcissem   invēnissem

mūtāveris	mōveris	trāxissēs	iēcissēs	invēnissēs
mūtāverit	mōverit	trāxisset	iēcisset	invēnisset
mūtāverimus	mōverimus	trāxissēmus	iēcissēmus	invēnissēmus
mūtāveritis	mōveritis	trāxissētis	iēcissētis	invēnissētis
mūtāverint	mōverint	trāxissent	iēcissent	invēnissent
mūtātus sim	mōtus sim	tractus essem	iactus essem	inventus essem
mūtātus sīs	mōtus sīs	tractus essēs	iactus esses	inventus essēs
mūtātus sit	mōtus sit	tractus esset	iactus esset	inventus esset
mūtātī sīmus	mōtī sīmus	tractī essēmus	iactī essemus	inventī essēmus
mūtātī sītis	mōtī sītis	tractī essētis	iactī essetis	inventī essētis
mūtātī sint	mōtī sint	tractī essent	iactī essent	inventī essent

4. asking   saying   knowing   perceiving   interrogatory   subjunctive
5.   present
                 perfect
                 imperfect
                 pluperferct
6. primary/principal   primary/principal secondary/historical   secondary/historical

DRILL

A. a. 1 pers sing perfect active
   b. 2 pers plur perfect active
   c. 2 pers sing imperfect active
   d. 2 pers plur present passive
   e. 1 pers sing pluperfect active
   f. 1 pers sing pluperfect passive
   g. 1 pers plur present active
   h. 2 pers plur imperfect active
   i. 2 pers sing present passive
   j. 1 pers plur imperfect active

   k. 2 pers sing perfect active
   l. 1 pers sing pluperfect active
   m. 1 pers sing perfect passive
   n. 2 pers plur pluperfect active
   o. 2 pers sing imperfect passive
   p. 2 pers plur imperfect passive
   q. 1 pers sing pluperfect passive
   r. 1 pers sing perfect active
   s. 2 pers plur pluperfect passive
   t. 1 pers sing perfect passive

B. a. inventa essent   He asked where the swords had been found.
   b. veniat   The world asks/is asking from where/whence evil comes/is coming.
   c. fūgerimus   The commanders will understand why we are fleeing/have fled/fled.
   d. vītarem   I had left to avoid the sun
   e. discessissem   My father explained why I had left.

C. a. Tanta/Tantum didicimus ut ōrātōrem comprehenderēmus.
   b. Discēmus cūr ōrātor comprehēnsus sit.
   c. Dux rogāvit unde mīlitēs vēnissent.
   d. Rogābit quandō ferrum ibi positum sit.

e. Scīs cūr signum nōn datum sit.

PRACTICE SENTENCES

a. I do not know where the money has been deposited.
b. Don't you know where the money will be/is deposited?
c. They knew where the money would be/was deposited.
d. He did not know where the money had been deposited.
e. The speaker asked why the remaining/rest of the citizens had not recognized these plans.
f. We heard that the citizens were so loyal that they preserved the republic.
g. We heard what the citizens had done to preserve the republic.
h. They used to ask in whose republic peace could be found/realized.
i. We learned that peace had not been found/realized in their country.
j. Those foolish men always ask what is better than supreme power or money.

CHAPTER 31

GRAMMAR

1. preposition	with		
2. when/after/once	because/since	although	nevertheless (tamen)
3. ferō	ferre	tulī	lātum
4. e	i	third	dūcō
5. ferō	feror	ferre	ferrī
fers	ferris	fer	
fert	fertur		
ferimus	ferimur		
fertis	feriminī	ferte	
ferunt	feruntur		

DRILL

A. a. to have carried
   b. to be about to carry
   c. having to be carried
   d. to have been carried
   e. 3 pers sing pluperfect active
   f. you carry
   g. you will be carried
   h. you are carried
   i. carry
   j. to be carried
   k. they carry
   l. they will carry
   m. 3 pers plur present active
   n. he is carried
   o. carry
   p. 3 pers sing present active
   q. he carries
   r. 3 pers sing imperfect active
   s. he will carry
   t. I had been carried

B. a. fuerit — Although (Though) he was ordinary/moderate/mediocre, we nevertheless tolerate him.
   b. mitterentur — When/After they were sent into exile, no help was provided.
   c. dētur — Although/Though wine is being given to you, nevertheless you are not enduring exile well.
   d. essētis — Because you were among enemies, friends went to you by ship.
   e. tulerant — After/Once they had provided help, we accomplished this in one year.

C. a. Cum tempora aequa essent, ferra tamen lāta sunt.
   b. Cum exsilium ducis iussum erat, discessērunt.
   c. Cum occāsiōnēs paucae essent, nāvēs parātae sunt.
   d. Cum discipilī expulsī essent, apud magistrum vēnērunt.
   e. Cum nāvis discēdit, maria aequa erunt.

PRACTICE SENTENCES

a. After we had said this, those men answered that they were about to offer an equitable peace.

b. Although he had gone to another country/land, he nevertheless found new friends.

c. Because they are offering us friendship, we shall offer them help.

d. Because the danger was great, they collected all the troops and arms in a short time.

e. After he had explained what he wanted, you said that so much help could not be given.

f. Although they had brought pleasing gifts, I nevertheless was able to recognize their treachery.

g. Because we now understand your plans, we shall not endure your treachery.

h. Although our soldiers had conquered the enemy, they nevertheless offered them many kindnesses.

i. Because/When he learned how many favors the rest were offering, he himself offered similar favors.

j. After the consul said these words, the senate replied that money had been collected for this purpose.

CHAPTER 32

GRAMMAR

1.
2. -e   -iter   -ly
3. -er
4. -ius   neuter   more   too   rather
5. -e   most   very

6. a. saepe   often   f. numquam   never
   b. semper   always   g. umquam   ever
   c. satis   enough   h. itaque   therefore
   d. nunc   now   i. autem   however
   e. tam   so   j. tamen   nevertheless

7. irregularities
8. nōlle   mālle   ne velle   magis velle   not to want/to be unwilling   to want more/to prefer

DRILL

A. a. pleasantly
   b. very faithfully/most loyally
   c. briefly
   d. worse
   e. rather/too faithfully/more loyally

   f. minimē
   g. longius/diutius
   h. male
   i. minus
   j. celerrimē

B. a. you will want
   b. you want
   c. you want
   d. they want
   e. he wants

   f. 1 pers plur present
   g. 1 pers plur imperfect
   h. 2 pers sing pluperfect
   i. you wanted
   j. 3 pers sing imperfect

C. a. celerrimē   The guards marched/went away very rapidly/swiftly.
   b. sapienter   We wisely preferred to have laws.
   c. vērē   The author had truly wanted to avoid either riches or honors.
   d. facillimē   We were very easily conquered by his army.
   e. celerius   The rich will want to acquire/have more riches too quickly/more rapidly.

D. a. Dīvitiās fēlīcissimē accēpērunt/cēpērunt/tulērunt.
   b. Discipulī nostrī celerius discent.
   c. Lēx/Iūs peius lēcta/lēctum est.
   d. Verba saepe acerbē/dūrē dīcuntur.
   e. Scientia semper clārissimē intellegenda/comprehenda est (comprehendī/intellegī debet).

PRACTICE SENTENCES

a. Certain people want to believe that all men are equal.
b. Certain people deny that the minds of all men are at least equal.
c. These men acquired/found wealth very rapidly; those men will be poor for a very long time.
d. This man wants to acquire very numerous/a very large number of honors as easily as possible.
e. We especially wish/want most to seek knowledge.
f. The citizens themselves ruled the republic better than that leader.
g. There the land is more level and is more accessible.
h. The tyrant was persecuting his citizens so badly that they always wanted to be free.
i. He will offer a very large number/multitude of gifts most freely in order that the army may be willing to help that tyrant.
j. He wants to accomplish these things more wisely in order not to lose even this opportunity.

CHAPTER 33

GRAMMAR

1. condition (protasis)   sī   if   nisi   if not/unless   conclusion (apodosis)
2. present   present

perfect	imperfect	perfect	imperfect
future	future perfect	future	
present	present		
imperfect	imperfect		
pluperfect	pluperfect		

3. future   present
4. should-would

DRILL

A. a. legātis   discātis   If you should read this, you would learn.
    b. lēgissētis   didicissētis   If you had read this, you would have learned.
    c. lēgistis/legēbātis   didicistis/discēbātis   If you read this, you learned.
                                                  If you were reading this, you were learning.
    d. lēgerētis   discerētis   If you were reading this, you would learn.
    e. legētis/lēgeritis   discētis   If you read this, you will learn.

B. a. Sī hōc/rem suscipitis/suscipiētis/suscēperis/suscēperitis, salūtem tradēs/tradetis.
    b. Sī hōc/rem suscipiās/suscipiātis, salūtem tradās/tradatis.
    c. Sī hōc/rem suscēpissēs/suscēpissētis, salūtem tradidissēs/tradidissētis.
    d. Sī h c/rem suscēpisī/suscepistis, salūtem tradidistī/tradidistis.
    e. Sī hōc/rem susciperēs/susciperētis, salūtem traderēs/traderētis.

PRACTICE SENTENCES

a. If reason prevails, you are happy.
b. If reason prevails, you will be happy.
c. If reason should prevail, you would be happy.
d. If reason were prevailing, you would be happy.
e. If reason had prevailed, you would have been happy.
f. If you love money, you lack wisdom.
g. If you love money, you will lack wisdom.
h. If you should love money, you would lack wisdom.
i. If you were loving money, you would lack wisdom.
j. If you had loved money, you would have lacked wisdom.
k. If we seek truth, we find knowledge.
l. If we seek truth, we shall find knowledge.

m. If we should seek truth, we would find knowledge.

n. If we were seeking truth, we would find knowledge.

o. If we had sought truth, we would have found knowledge.

CHAPTER 34

GRAMMAR

1. to lay/set aside/to depose   passive   active   participles   infinitives

   present   future   future   future

2. loquens, ntis   speaking   locūtus, a, um   having spoken

   locuturus, a, um   about to speak   loquendus, a, um   having to be spoken

3. ūtī   to use

   ūsus, a, um   to have used

   usūrus, a, um esse   to be about to use

4. cōnāris (re)   you try/are trying/do try

   cōnāberis (re)   you will try

   cōnābāris (re)   you were trying/used to try

   cōnātus, a, um es   you tried, have tried, did try

   cōnātus, a, um eris   you will have tried

   cōnātus, a, um erās   you had tried

   cōnēris (re)

   cōnārēris (re)

   cōnātus, a, um sis

   cōnātus, a, um essēs

5. ēgredereleavego out

   ēgrediminīleavego out

6. passive

7. ablative   accusative   reflexive

DRILL

A. a. to be about to use

   b. you will suffer

   c. 3 pers sing pluperfect

   d. you suffer

   e. having used

   f. suffer/you suffer

   g. 3 pers sing imperfect

   h. to suffer

   i. he uses

   j. they suffered

   k. 3 pers sing present

   l. to have suffered

   m. he will use

   n. suffering

   o. it mustought to be endured

   p. 3 pers sing present

   q. he suffers

   r. we shall suffer

   s. 3 pers sing imperfect

   t. 3 pers sing present

B. a. proficīscēmur   We shall set out for/proceed to the island.

   b. ūsī/ūsae sunt   They used water.

   c. cōnābar   I was attempting to save the girls.

   d. secūtī/secūtae erant   They had followed him into exile.

   e. patienda   The evils must be endured by them.

C. a. Moritūrus loquī ausus est

   b. Insulā saepe ūsī/ūsae sumus ut salūtem nostram cōnservārēmus.

   c. Urbe profectī, hostēs secūtī sunt.

   d. Aquā frūctibusque illīus insulae ūtuntur.

e. Illā/Eā nocte fīlius eius apud amīcum nātus est.

PRACTICE SENTENCES

a. He believes that these misfortunes must be endured.
b. We shall try to endure these misfortunes.
c. Unless you wish to die, endure these misfortunes.
d. Having endured the greatest misfortunes, the poor man died.
e. After these words were uttered, we dared to follow him.
f. After we spoke these words, we set out so as not to die in this wretched place.
g. If someone should dare to use wine of this kind, he would die quickly.
h. On the same day, his son was born and he died.
i. Let's use all our recources to save our country.
j. If they had used better books, they would have learned more.

CHAPTER 35

GRAMMAR

1. dative	accusative		
2. to	noun	pronoun	dative
3. is not	prefix	preposition	dative

DRILL

A. a. eum/eam/id — They recognize himherit
   b. eī — They forgive himher
   c. eī — They serve himher
   d. eum/eam/id — They save himherit
   e. eum/eam/id — They tolerate himherit
   f. eum/eam/id — They will find himherit
   g. eī — They harm himherit
   h. eī — They please himher
   i. id — They throw it
   j. eī — They believe himherit
   k. eō/eā — They lack himherit
   l. eum/eam — They urge himher
   m. eum/eam/id — They follow himherit
   n. eī — They persuade himher
   o. eō/eā — They use himherit

B. a. Lēgem — I understand the law.
   b. Reī pūblicae — They harmed the republic.
   c. Exercitū — We used the army.
   d. Servīs — I commanded the slaves.
   e. mihi — The reward pleases me.

C. a. Lēgī pāreāmus.
   b. Custōdiae eī bene servīvērunt.
   c. Auctōrī persuāsērunt.
   d. Exercitus nūllīs opibus pepercit
   e. Pater fīliō suō īgnōscit.

PRACTICE SENTENCES

a. The slaves serve other men.
b. That slave served my son and saved him.
c. If someone had undertaken this task, he would have saved many people.

d. If we want God to forgive us, we must forgive other men.
e. They do not believe me now, nor will they ever be willing to believe my son.
f. Since you lacked good faith, they could not believe you.
g. Let us obey this commander so that he may spare us and save the city.
h. Unless Caesar pleases the citizens, they will not spare his life.
i. Let us always consider and obey truth and wisdom.
j. Always consider the best things if you truly wish to be happy.

CHAPTER 36

GRAMMAR
1. indirect discourse
2. indirect statement   infinitive   nominative   accusative   that
3. indirect question   subjunctive   interrogatory
4. hortatory subjunctive imperative   jussive subjunctive
5. infinitive   jussive purpose purpose   noun   ut   nē   subjunctive
6. ōrō   rogō   hortōr   moneō   imperō   persuadeō   (petō   quaerō)

DRILL
A. a. having to be made/done/become
   b. 1 pers plur present
   c. They will be made/done/become
   d. 1 pers sing imperfect
   e. 3 pers plur present
   f. they are made/done/become
   g. we use to be made/done/become
   h. you will be made/done/become
   i. to have been made/done/become
   j. 3 pers plur imperfect

   k. he will be made/done/become
   l. it is made/he becomes
   m. 3 pers sing present
   n. 2 pers plur imperfect
   o. to be made/done/become
   p. 1 pers plur perfect
   q. 1 pers sing present/I shall make
   r. we madehave madedid make
   s. 2 pers sing pluperfect
   t. you will have been made/become

B. a. nocērent   We persuaded them not to harm him/her.
   b. accēdant   I urge them to approach.
   c. ignōsceret   I had asked her to forgive me.
   d. fieret   He ordered him not to become too powerful.
   e. pāream   Are you warning me to obey you?

C. a. Eī persuādē ut dux fīat.
   b. Eum monē nē metum/timōrem habeat.
   c. Eī imperāvērunt ut praemium acciperet.
   d. Fēmina a filiā suā petīvit nē discēderet.
   e. Eos hortātī sumus ut sine timōre/metū īnsidiās fatērentur.

PRACTICE SENTENCES
a. He said that they studied Latin literature.
b. He told why they studied Latin literature.
c. He spoke in order that they might study Latin literature.
d. I am asking you why you did this.
e. I am asking you to do this.
f. I beg you in order that peace be made.
g. They were begging me not to make war.
h. I beseeched him not to obey the evil king.
i. We beg you to become very sharp students.
j. Take care to do this.

CHAPTER 37

GRAMMAR

1. i e a o u present present present participle gerund
2. is not curo
3. ab (a) de ex (e) ablative
   in ablative
   in or ad accusative (motion)
4. genitive ablative
   genitive ablative
   ablative ablative
5. none locative
   none ablative
   none accusative
6. none ablative
   none ablative
   none accusative

DRILL

A. a. we went
   b. 1 pers plur imperfect
   c. 1 pers plur pluperfect
   d. 1 pers plur present
   e. they went
   f. we used to go
   g. to be about to go
   h. going
   i. they go/are goingdo go
   j. they will go

B. a. for one day
   b. one day/in one day
   c. in Rome
   d. for many days
   e. to Rome
   f. into/on the ship
   g. home
   h. in A/thens/from Athens
   i. at home
   j. to A/thens
   k. from home
   l. in the ship

C. a. Athēnīs — My brother departed from A/thens.
   b. Romām — He/She is going to Rome.
   c. Domō — He/She had departed from home.
   d. Athēnās — Next, he returned to Athens.
   e. domī — Finally, let us perish at home.

D. a. Amīcī meī ūnā hōrā domō abiērunt.
   b. Paucōs diēs Rōmae remanēbunt/manēbunt.
   c. Unō diē Athēnās redeāmus.
   d. Illō/Eō diē ad īnsulam ībit.
   e. Dīcat/Licet dīcere eōs celeriter redīsse.

PRACTICE SENTENCES

a. In a few hours, we shall go to Rome.
b. We are going to the city they are going home.
c. Why did you leave home so quickly?
d. They are coming to Rome to go to Athens with my brother.
e. Depart this city to (go) to (your) death and perish in order that I may not perish.
f. After your brother had been killed in Rome, they returned to Athens.
g. He denied that he wanted to stay in that land for many days.
h. You said that you were about to return home from Athens within one hour.
i. During those days, we were accustomed to being in Athens.
j. If they had harmed his friends in Rome, he would have returned to Rome in a very short time.

CHAPTER 38

GRAMMAR
1. fact

2.
quī	quae	quod	quī	quae	quae
cuius	cuius	cuius	cuius	cuius	cuius
cui	cui	cui	cui	cui	cui
quem	quam	quod	quōs	quās	quae
quō	quā	quō	quibus	quibus	quibus

3. a. purpose   d. cum
   b. result   e. conditional
   c. indirect question   f. jussive noun (indirect command)
4. characteristic   general   indefinite   interrogative   negative

5. a. There are people/men who
   b. There are women who/things which
   c. Who is there who?
   d. What is there which?
   e. There is no one who
   f. There is nothing which
   g. He is the only one who

6. essential   complementary   completing   verb   emotional effect

7. a. In your opinion, must we return home?
   b. As you see it, must we return home?
   c. In your view, must we return home?

DRILL
A. a. sentiat   She is the only one who feels hatred.
   b. sit   Who is there whose destiny/fate is certain?
   c. facit   The girl who is accomplishing the task is there.
   d. cōnsūmerētur   In your opinion, there was no one who was being consumed with hatred.
   e. amat   My brother who loves me will defend me.

B. a. Sunt quī īgnōscere nōn dubitent.
   b. Sunt paucī quī dolōrem nōn metuant.
   c. Quis est quī auctōritātem eius dubitet?
   d. Cīvēs quī auctōritātem eius dubitābant dīmissī sunt.
   e. Sōlī erant quī pedibus ūterentur.

PRACTICE SENTENCES
a. But there used to be no one who defended that evil man.
b. What is there which men fear more than a tyrant?
c. Who is there who hesitates between freedom and domination by a tyrant?
d. In ancient Rome, there were those who loved money more than the republic.
e. Who is there who can suffer such great pain?
f. I know nothing which can, in my view, be easier.
g. I am seeking the sort of leader whom everyone praises/all men praise.
h. I am seeking that great leader whom everyone praises.
i. In the view of ancient men, there was nothing which was better than courage and wisdom.
j. Nothing must be feared which cannot harm the soul.

CHAPTER 39

GRAMMAR

1. verbal adjective   verb   adjective
2. adjective   ½
3. verbal noun   verb   noun
4. noun   second   neuter   active infinitive present
5. vīvere   living/to live

   vīvendī   of living

   vīvendō   to/for living

   vīvendum   living

   vīvendō   by/with/from living

6.   We learn by reading books with care.

librīs legendīs   We learn by reading books with care.

DRILL

A. a. gerundive
   b. gerund
   c. gerundive
   d. gerund
   e. gerund
   f. gerundive
   g. gerundive
   h. gerund
   i. gerundive
   j. gerund

B. a. videndī   We were eager for the building to be seen.
   b. scrībendī   The art of writing was being praised.
   c. scrībendōs   This was said against writing verses.
   d. petendam   They will come to seek/petition for/sue for peace.
   e. eundī   The fear of going home was real.

C. a. Vōcis tuae/vestrae audiendae causā vēnimus.
   b. Legere necesse est.
   c. Post litterās legendās eum vīdērunt.
   d. Legendō sapientēs fīmus.
   e. Prō urbe līberandā locūtus est.

PRACTICE SENTENCES

a. We learn by trying.
b. He devoted himself to learning.
c. For the sake of learning, they came to your school.
d. The fear of dying was frightening him.
e. The hope of living after death sustains many people.
f. He conquered them by scheming.
g. He devoted himself to learning Latin literature.
h. He wrote a book about defending freedom.
i. We become wiser by experiencing life.
j. He took up a lot of time in performing these tasks.

CHAPTER 40

GRAMMAR

1. genitive   genitive   whole   partitive genitive
2. nouns   pronouns   adjectives
3. second   adjective
4. four   100   mille   indeclinable
5. ūnus   duo   trēs   200   900   declinable
6. mīlia   i-stem noun   third   genitive   whole
7. quīdam   ex   dē   ablative
8. first   second

9.

duo	duae	duo	trēs	trēs	tria
duōrum	duārum	duōrum	trium	trium	trium
duōbus	duābus	duōbus	tribus	tribus	tribus
duōs	duās	duo	trēs	trēs	tria
duōbus	duābus	duōbus	tribus	tribus	tribus

10.

ūnīus	ūnīus	ūnīus
ūnī	ūnī	ūnī

DRILL

A. a. ten citizens
    b. three out of six citizens
    c. a hundred citizens
    d. one hundred of the citizens
    e. three thousand citizens
    f. a certain one of the citizens
    g. which hope?
    h. less fear
    i. no water
    j. enough assistance

B. a. vōcēs   A thousand voices will be heard.
    b. vōcum   Many thousands of voices will be heard.
    c. Duo   We do not have two heads.
    d. Tertium   They will discover a third man.
    e. septem   Seven years later, they returned.

C. a. Quattuor ex servīs tribus dominīs servīvērunt.
    b. Unus dē dominīs scit.
    c. Mīlle hominēs dīmittere necesse est.
    d. Auctor quattuordecim versūs scrīpsit.
    e. Quārtum decimum versum lēgī.

PRACTICE SENTENCES

a. Hello, my friend. What are you doing?/How do you do? What's new?
b. Greetings to you too./hello to you also. Well. Nothing new.
c. Do you want to hear something good? I finally received/gained enough wealth/riches.
d. But what good is there in riches alone? Do you also have enough wisdom?
e. However, most rich men feel much fear.
f. The poor are often happier and have less fear.
g. Nine of the commanders urged us to provide more assistance.
h. He will never have enough leisure yet some leisure is better than nothing.
i. Nowadays/In our time, we all have too much fear and too little hope.
j. Great faith and courage must be found by all men.